# Timeless Writings - 30

## Tatay Jobo Elizes
### Compiler
### 2017

# Published by Tatay Jobo Elizes, Self-Publisher

This book is published and printed under the expressed permission of the various authors compiled for this purpose of making their articles and essays available to the public and promote reading among Filipinos, young and old. They own the copyrights to their writings. Authors can withdraw or rescind their permission anytime and will be edited out in next printing. Printing of this book is using the present day method of Print-On-Demand (POD) or Book-On-Demand (BOD) systems, where prints will never run out of copies. Authors are free to republish or reprint with other publishers and printers anytime.

## ISBN Codes

ISBN – 13: 978 – 1542602679    and
ISBN – 10: 154260267X

Disclaimer: Views are expressed by the authors alone. Tatay Jobo Elizes does not knowingly publish false information or commit copyright infringement having been given explicit permission to publish this book. Tatay Jobo Elizes may not be held liable for the views of the authors exercising their right to free expression.

## Self-Publisher's Details:

Contact: job_elizes@yahoo.com
Websites:   http:tinyurl.com/mj76ccq +
www.jobelizes6.wix.com/mysite

# Contents

# 1.

## The Roots of Crisis: A Neo-Colonial State

### BY ALEJANDRO LICHAUCO
### *Posted by Bulatlat*

**The sovereign nationhood was pure fiction because the colonial power which supposedly returned to us the independence which it had wrested from Bonifacio's revolution never really left and never really allowed us to exist and act as a free and sovereign people.**

Any attempt to understand the essence and roots of the nation's crisis must begin with recognition of the nature of the Philippine state. The Philippines isn't - and one must stress that - a sovereign, independent state that it is assumed to be and which its constitution claims it is.

### A neocolonial state

The Philippines is a neocolonial state - which, by definition, means a state that is sovereign and independent in theory but which in fact is the colony of another, or of others. As a people, we are the classic victim of what Webster's New World Dictionary calls neocolonialism and which it defines as "the exploitation of a supposedly independent nation as by imposing a puppet government."

This has been so from the day and moment that we assumed the status of sovereign nationhood in 1946. That sovereign nationhood was pure fiction. It was pure fiction because the colonial power which supposedly returned to us the independence which it had wrested from Bonifacio's revolution never really left and never really allowed us to exist and act as a free and sovereign people.

The process by which we have been preserved as a neo-colony is a story of its own, and neither time nor space allows that I deal with it in detail. It should suffice to focus on the essentials of that process. We have been preserved as a neocolonial state through the flagrant and systematic intervention of the U.S. government in our political process and in the creation of a collaborator class.

Neocolonialist intervention, of course, hasn't been confined to the political process. You see and feel the hand of that intervention in just about every aspect of Philippine society and the political economy. You see and feel it not only in government and politics but in the business community, in our schools, civil society, media and even the churches.

But the intervention has been most crucial and fatal at the level of our presidential politics. As the late and former President Diosdado Macapagal admitted in an article he wrote for the Bulletin a few years before he passed away, the U.S. government has been a decisive factor in every presidential election since 1935, and no presidential aspirant objectionable to Washington has ever been elected president. By the same token, any sitting president who manages to displease Washington invariably winds up unseated by Washington. That has been generally the fate of all incumbent presidents. They were mounted to office by Washington and eventually unseated by Washington.

That's how puppet governments are mounted and that's essentially how we have been preserved as a neocolonial state.

But that's for another paper. At the moment we are focused on the economic crisis.

### The fiscal crisis: a diversionary issue

The fiscal crisis, which you invited me to discuss, is in truth only one of the many facets of the economic crisis that grips the nation. There is the crisis of the peso, the crisis of unemployment and inflation; there is the crisis of the industrial and agricultural sectors, and there is the overall crisis of underdevelopment and poverty.

There is the crisis of the very economic system by which we have lived all these years.

To be lured into a discussion of the fiscal crisis therefore is to be lured away from a discussion of the totality of the crisis and the nature as well as the root of that crisis. And that I suggest to you is exactly what the enemies of the state intend. They intend to lure us away from an examination of the total crisis and to trivialize that crisis by luring us into a discussion of what they call the "fiscal-debt crisis."

But it is the essence and root of the total economic crisis that we should focus on.

### The economic crisis of a neocolonial state

If we have a total economic crisis in our hands - a crisis whose most visible and terrifying manifestation is the mass hunger, and not only the mass poverty, that now grips the land and which government itself has acknowledged - it is because in this post-industrial age, we remain a nation of 80 million mired in the pre-industrial stage of history.

The question is: Why have we remained stuck in the pre-industrial age of history when neighbors once more impoverished and backward than we are have either graduated, or are dramatically in the process of graduating, into the age of science and industry?

And the answer is that it has been planned that way. From the beginning, it was planned in Washington that the Philippines shall remain essentially a raw material economy in order to service the raw material requirements of an industrial Japan.

### The Dodds Report

In 1946, the Truman administration adopted the recommendation of the report which proposed that Japan be developed as the primary, if not sole, industrial powerhouse in the Asia-Pacific region and that countries like the Philippines should be preserved as raw material economies, obviously to service the requirements of Japan's factories.

As the Asia-Pacific war came to a close, the U.S. obviously made a fateful decision to utilize Japan as the base from which to project U.S. military power, and that required the development of Japan as an industrial powerhouse. But since Japan is a nation bereft of natural resource, the plan obviously required that countries like the Philippines be preserved as raw material economics to ensure Japan with a continuing and permanent source of raw material.

We owe our knowledge of the Dodds Report to the late Salvador Araneta who, during his self-exile in Canada during the martial law years, uncovered the existence of the document and denounced it in his book *America's Double-Cross of the Philippines*.

These were Araneta's denunciatory words, as he explained the failure of the nation to industrialize: "The indifferent economic development of the country ... was due to America's policy toward Japan and the Philippines. This policy was the result of the Dodds Report which Truman accepted and which had as its objective to make Japan the industrial workshop of Asia and the Philippines a mere supplier of raw materials."

As Araneta bitterly continued: "We do not argue against the wisdom of providing Japan with the means to rehabilitate herself and allowed to become an industrial country once again, although this was contrary to the    prior recommendation of a post-war planning committee headed by Secretary Morgenthau, a recommendation which was in line with the prevailing sentiment at the end of the war. But certainly we can argue against a policy that would make Japan the exclusive industrialized country in the Far East, for such a policy was most detrimental to the Philippines. Indeed, the United States could not justify a policy that provided all kinds of stumbling blocks, to the industrialization of her ally (Philippines) in the war against Japan. As a result of this policy, industrialization in the Philippines suffered severe setbacks…"

It was a division of labor, or of functions, which the Dodds, Report crafted for America's allies in the Far East.

The Dodds Report explains the continuing obsession to this day of U.S. foreign policy to keep the Philippines a free and open market for imports because a liberal import policy - another name for free trade - ensures that this country will never be able to industrialize and take the same protectionist, nationalistic developmental strategy that enabled once poorer neighbors like Taiwan, Malaysia and Thailand, to transform into the newly industrialized countries that they are today.

The geopolitical plan embodied in the Dodds Report explains what the late Claro M. Recto described as "America's anti?industrialization policy for the Philippines."

Although Recto had no knowledge of the existence of the Dodds Report at the time - its existence would surface only in the 1970s after Araneta exposed it - his enormous analytical power enabled him to deduce from policy statements of U.S. officials that behind U.S. policy in this country was a malevolent design to see to it that we never industrialize.

Conclusive proof of what Recto described as America's "anti-industrialization policy for the Philippines" came when Marcos formally launched an industrialization program in the late '70s based on 11 heavy industries led by the steel, petrochemical and engineering industries.

The announcement of that plan was swiftly followed by protest from the IMF and the World Bank and the pro-American technocrats in the Marcos cabinet led by no less than his then Prime Minister.

In the end, after four years of struggle with the IMF, the World Bank and his own technocrats over his industrialization plan, Marcos gave up the plan but not until after he had expressly denounced a conspiracy between his own technocrats and the IMF-WB to keep the Philippines under the heels of the industrial powers.

Soon after his election to the presidency, Joseph Estrada in an interview with Asiaweek confirmed that the U.S. has indeed sabotaged the industrialization plan of Marcos.

The U.S. anti-industrialization policy for the Philippines is what those IMF conditionalities are really about. The anti-industrialization policy has been implemented all these years through the IMF conditionalities and it isn't any coincidence that for the last forty years this country has been under the continuous economic supervision of the IMF. There is no country in the world that can claim to be under the supervision of the IMF for even a fraction of that time.

And it isn't coincidence either that this country, which has been under the continuous supervision of the IMF for 40 years, is the only country in the region that isn't making any headway toward industrialization.

When the Asean was founded in the early 160s by the Philippines, Malaysia, Thailand, Indonesia and Singapore, not a single one of them was an NIC.

Today, only the Philippines remains outside the magic circle of NICs. The four other co-founders of the Asean are now acknowledged NICs.

That should explain why the Philippines has the longest and oldest communist insurgency in the region.

A nation of 80 million without even the capability to produce a decent hammer or a decent toy gun can't possibly have any future except hunger.

We are today a hungry people in a land so fertile that one can drop a seed anywhere and see it sprout into something he can eat. And we are hungry because we are a nation frozen by design in the pre-industrial age, preserved as a raw material economy.

The essence and root of our crisis, to stress, are to be found in the nature of the Philippines as a neocolonial state preserved by U.S. post-war imperialism as a raw material economy to service the raw material requirements of an industrial Japan.

### The treason of the Edsa Constitution

The ultimate tragedy of a neocolonial state is that even its own Constitution becomes an instrument of its own and perpetual enslavement.

And the Philippine case is a classic illustration.

I invite your attention to Art. XII, Sec. 1, par. 2 of the Constitution which reads as follows: "The State shall promote industrialization and full employment based on sound agricultural development and agrarian reform through industries that make full and efficient use of human and natural resources, and which are competitive in both domestic and foreign markets. However, the State shall protect Filipino enterprises against unfair foreign competition and trade practices."

That provision you will note automatically prohibits an industrial policy based on the heavy industries and the application of protectionist measures against foreign competition, whether fair or unfair.

While the provision stipulates that the "State shall promote industrialization" it simultaneously qualifies that constitutional directive with an entire complex of conditions and limiting reservations which makes it impossible for the State to adopt any industrialization strategy other than one that is specifically and exclusively based on "sound agricultural development and agrarian reform" whatever that means.

For example, the provision literally prohibits an industrialization strategy based on the heavy industries, like steel, chemicals, machine tools and machine production. But that's precisely the kind of strategy that made NICS of our neighbors.

Our neighbors - particularly South Korea and Taiwan - didn't transform into newly- industrialized countries through the industrialization strategy explicitly mandated by the above-cited provision of our Constitution. Those countries, imitating Japan, pursued an industrialization strategy anchored on the development of industries based on and moved by machine power rather than on "sound agricultural development and agrarian reform."

A real industrialization program is one that is based on what is known as the capital goods industry - industries based on machine power and the production of what is known as the means of production.

Any other industrialization program can only be a program based on light consumer industries that are totally dependent on industrial raw material and industrial machines produced by the industrialized countries.

You will further note that the constitutional provision insists that industries should be competitive in both the domestic and foreign markets. With that provision, there is hardly any industry that can qualify for government support and protection, and that is precisely what the provision intends. That provision serves as justification for our reckless entry into GATT and the equally reckless accelerated tariff reduction program of the government - programs which have contributed heavily to the bankruptcy of National Steel Corporation, the closure of Caltex refinery and the financial problems of an enterprise like Hacienda Luisita, all of whom have attributed their crisis to the flood of imports unleashed by the government's commitments to the WTO.

No country rose from rags to riches through industrialization by exposing its industries to foreign competition the way we have done. Examine the industrial policies of the Asian NICs and you will see how protective those policies are of their basic industries, even if these are not competitive in the foreign markets.

While the constitutional provision does provide that the State shall protect Filipino enterprises against unfair foreign competition, it doesn't define what unfair foreign competition means. For example, we have exposed our agricultural sector to competition from subsidized agricultural imports, but the authorities don't consider that a contravention of the Constitution. The result is that even the agricultural sector has been marginalized. Apparently, the authorities see nothing wrong with pitting our farmers, most of whom hardly made it to sixth grade, with the corporate farmers of the industrial countries, who do their farming with the aid of satellites.

The authorities must be reminded that any underdeveloped economy struggling to industrialize would have to protect its basic industries from foreign competition, whether fair or unfair. To insist that even infant industries should be competitive in the foreign markets would be tantamount to killing these infant industries from the start.

The question is: Why did the authors of the present Constitution feel it necessary to qualify the industrialization mandate with the kind of restrictions they placed on it?

And the answer is that the authors of the cited provision were the very elements who had opposed the heavy industrialization program launched by Ferdinand Marcos in 1979. The Marcos industrial program was based the establishment of industries driven by machine power and not - repeat, not - by "sound agricultural development and agrarian reform" as stipulated by the present Constitution.

In brief, no less than the Constitution has become the barrier to the real industrialization of our economy. Under the "industrialization" provision of the Charter there isn't any way that this country can transform into a newly industrialized country or NIC. Which means that there isn't any way we can get out of the poverty trap which has now mutated into a hunger crisis.

Article XII, Sec. 1 Par. 2 of the Constitution is the best evidence of our status as neocolonial state. It is also the ultimate weapon which ensures that the anti-industrialization agenda of the Dodds Report will remain unchallenged by any government elected under the present charter.

If by some miracle we should have a government tomorrow bent on industrializing the economy by adopting the same industrial policies that have made industrialized countries of our neighbors, such a government would run afoul of the Constitution.

What then is to be done?

Complete the unfinished nationalist revolution of Bonifacio.

What needs to be done is clearly to forge a national coalition of forces committed to recovering the sovereignty which American imperialism wrested from Bonifacio's revolution and to transform the Philippines from the neocolonial state that it is to the truly sovereign and independent state that it claims to be and should be.

Only when the Philippines becomes a truly sovereign and independent state can it then proceed to pursue the kind of developmental policies necessary to lift the economy out of the pre-industrial age of history and to catapult it to the ranks of newly industrialized countries.

Three processes that should be unleashed if social peace is to be achieved.

Such a coalition could be forged on the basis of a program that would unleash three vital processes, namely: The process of decolonization, the process of industrialization and the process of economic democratization.

Only when these three processes are unleashed simultaneously, through a program of government crafted specifically for that purpose, can the nation begin the journey towards social peace. The reason is that social peace can only come with social justice and economic democracy. But social justice and economic democracy can come about only if there is economic development, and economic development can come about only with an industrial revolution which in turn can come about only with national independence.

I propose accordingly that no time be lost organizing a national coalition based on a program that would unleash the three processes of de-colonization, industrialization and economic democratization.

In 1986, I proposed such a program to the then ongoing Constitutional Commission - which that body completely ignored. I now propose that that program be adopted as a working basis of dialogue among all elements in Philippine society determined to transform the Philippines into a truly sovereign and independent state so that it may proceed with the war on mass poverty and thereby pave the way for the much longed social peace which has long eluded us.

That program is embodied in a slim volume I authored titled Towards a New Economic Order and the Conquest of Mass Poverty, and which I incorporate by reference in this paper. That program, incidentally, is a synthesis of the basic principles found in the program of the Movement for the Advancement of Nationalism and the Vatican encyclicals which condemn laissez-faire capitalism and justify on moral grounds the principle of state activism in the economy.

Along with the program outlined in Towards a New Economic Order and the Conquest of Mass Poverty, I recommend the adoption, as a working basis of dialogue, an emergency program of government proposed by the Citizens Committee on the National Crisis last January, which I also incorporate by way of reference.

We must complete Bonifacio's unfinished revolution if we are to face up to the crisis that has made this only Christian nation in Asia a humanitarian disaster, where 80 percent of Filipino households live under hunger conditions. The imperatives of national survival and the revolution against hunger which has now overtaken us call for nothing less than the revolutionary nationalism which forged Filipinos into one nation.

Only when the country commits itself to a program of government that would unleash the three processes of de-colonization, industrialization and economic democratization can it begin the march toward social peace because only a government committed to the unleashing of those three processes would have the credibility to deal with the insurgents and the secessionists.

That is one way of saying that the road to social peace begins with the struggle to regain the sovereignty and independence which U.S. imperialism stole from Bonifacio's revolution.

That sovereignty and independence should be recovered at all cost if we are to survive as a viable society.

One final and concluding note.

### Debt repudiation

There isn't any way we can proceed to retrieve our sovereignty and independence unless we first repudiate the foreign debt. The repudiation of that debt should be the starting point of any genuine effort at national independence and sovereignty.

I have written the Senate a letter-memorandum outlining the case for unconditional debt repudiation and I incorporate that letter-memorandum to this paper by way of reference.

I suggest that the Pilgrims for Peace initiate a signature campaign urging the Senate to adopt the letter-memorandum for debt repudiation. Such a campaign could well serve as the catalyst for a nationwide coalition that would complete the unfinished revolution.

### The principal contradiction

The contradiction between colonialism and nationalism remains the principal contradiction of Philippine society. To the resolution of that contradiction all other contradictions should be subordinated.

The road to peace starts with that. It starts with the drive to eliminate colonialism in all its forms and from whatever source.

Recto, the consummate Filipino nationalist and Mao, the consummate Chinese Communist, will shake hands on that.

**Posted by Bulatlat**

*Paper for the Pilgrims for Peace Forum Quezon City Oct. 27, 2004*

---oOo---

# 2.

## 100 Days in Dutertopia

### Clinton Palanca

*Clinton Palanca has won awards for his fiction and in 1998, came out with Landscapes, a book compiling his short stories and earlier works for children. Today, he ventures into food writing with his regular column on In-quirer Lifestyle, and with restaurant reviews for other publications.*

**Dateline, Oct. 7, 2016**
**Phil Esquire Magazine, online**
**(by courtesy & attribution)**

*The most popular president in living memory has just passed his first milestone. What the first three months has revealed about Duterte as a leader, and about us as a nation, truly, frightening.*

How long must we go on being outraged? This is not a rhetorical question: being outraged is hard work. We wake up in the morning, check our social media feeds, check the news, read the comments sections. Our blood begins to boil. We feel rage, frustration, and helplessness. But the day's work must be done, and so we put our feelings on the back burner and go about our business, until something else—the futility of sitting in traffic, the mendacity of the clerks at the post office, the indignity of being sideswiped by a black SUV bristling with bumper stickers declaring their love of guns and allegiance to the new president—reminds us that we now live in Dutertopia. If the Japanese have kaizen, the philosophy of continuous improvement, we have the opposite, whatever it is called: things just get worse every day.

The news is not good. At the top of the list are the extrajudicial killings, often abbreviated snazzily as "EJK," which makes it sound harmless, like a medical condition. But to press a point, ours is a country without a death penalty, so there is no such thing as a judicial killing. These are murders, pure and simple. They continue, every day; many news outlets have been keeping a running tally. This, and other aspects of Mr. Duterte's obsession with drugs and drug addicts in general, are chilling. He has said, during the State of the Nation address, no less, that methamphetamine addicts have shrunken brains and are beyond rehabilitation. Drug addicts, furthermore, are "contagious" and turn into pushers who get their friends hooked on drugs. Photos of overcrowded prisons have started to circulate, which further bolsters his solution: to simply kill them, like carriers of a plague.

*The news is not good. At the top of the list are the extrajudicial killings, often abbreviated snazzily as "EJK," which makes it sound harmless, like a medical condition. These are murders, pure and simple. They continue, every day.*

We tend to think that our friends think like us: that's why they're our friends, after all. So when intelligent, kind, generous people, with whom we have shared many meals and laughter, declare that they are not just okay with the new politics of violence, but that it's good for the country, we can't help but feel betrayed. It's like discovering that they believe the world is flat. And then we begin to discover that more people than we think believe that this president is a great man, and that what he is doing is beneficial and the sight of a dead "drug lord" is a beautiful thing. This is the point at which we begin to wonder if we're the only sane people left in the country, and whether the walls of the madhouse are to hold us in or keep the world outside.

This is the dark side of our people's ability to quickly form collective movements; 30 years ago the empathetic euphoria took on a dictator, successfully, and was given the term "People Power." It is the same ability to convince ourselves and others that gave a candidate, who won with less than 40 percent of the official vote, the mandate of a 91 percent trust rating in a survey done shortly after his proclamation.

*And then we begin to discover that more people than we think believe that this president is a great man, and that what he is doing is beneficial and the sight of a dead "drug lord" is a beautiful thing. This is the point at which we begin to wonder if we're the only sane people left in the country, and whether the walls of the madhouse are to hold us in or keep the world outside.*

Even by the standards of a newly elected president, these are high numbers. The presidential communications team has had no hesitation in trumpeting these numbers to their advantage, nor in casting detractors as an #Enemy of Change. (The coming polling numbers in October is likely to bring a less buoyant vision, but the more ardent supporters can be somewhat selective in their choice of which facts to highlight.)

Since then, Mr. Duterte has parlayed his political capital into a public acceptance of his war on drugs; he has overcome formidable resistance both in government and in the populace to allow Marcos's burial in the National Heroes' Cemetery; and he's begun a process of charter change that would break the Philippines up into self-governing states (i.e., federalism) and change the government to a parliamentary system, albeit one with an elected president. He has also goaded the military to try and come at him with a coup d'etat, threatened to impose Martial Law in response to a rebuke by the Supreme Court, and called the U.S. ambassador a putangina on public television.

*At a certain point all the handwringing eventually peters away, because our wrists are exhausted; all the keyboard warriors stop typing because their fingers are numb; all the voices of dissent stop shouting because there's no one shouting with them.*

Fewer people (than one would have thought) are disturbed by this. At a rally against the Marcos burial only a few thousand—reported by the New York Times as "hundreds"—showed up, an embarrassingly poor showing that further weakened the opposition. At a certain point all the handwringing eventually peters away, because our wrists are exhausted; all the keyboard warriors stop typing because their fingers are numb; all the voices of dissent stop shouting because there's no one shouting with them.

This gradual acceptance of the status quo is a slow plummet to the bottom. Only automatons can go on without a break; only true zealots don't stop to question themselves. We begin to wonder if popular wisdom has been right all along. Perhaps this really is what the country needs. Human rights are for sissies and the squeamish, and a purge is a necessary sacrifice to rid the country of the twin vices of drugs and corruption. We have been blind, so blind all along, to how China and the previous administration was turning this country into a narco-state. It's probably just rival gangs offing one another, so even if it's bloody it'll be the good guys who are left standing. The US and other prim finger-wagging first world countries know nothing of the realities of our grinding poverty and the grim reality of drug use that have broken up families and turned good men into murderers.

*This gradual acceptance of the status quo is a slow plummet to the bottom. Only automatons can go on without a break; only true zealots don't stop to question themselves.*

When frustration and futility turn to indifference, the self-justification starts to kick in. Look, Marcos's body isn't even a body, it's just a wax figurine, and it's all just symbolic, after all. Let it be done, so we can get on with our lives. Allow the president his personal obsession if he can deliver on his promises to instill the fear of God in the predatory government bureaux who make our lives hell. Maybe he'll even succeed, and heaven knows, there is nothing to like about crystal meth. This is change worth pursuing. How wonderful, how blissful it feels to surrender, to stop fi ghting it, to accept the premises of Dutertopia. It feels, ironically, like letting morphine course through the body: no more anger, no more frustration, let daddy take care of things. He's on your side and he'll keep the bad people away.

In a warped, oddball way, this is finally the idea-based politics that the Philippines has been lacking. We don't actually have a divide between Democrat and Republican, between Liberal and Conservative, between far-right and socialist. Yes, our parties do have platforms, perfunctorily, but our election politics is largely personality-based. But the main fault line in our democracy is the polarization between people who believe in government institutions who operate within a system of checks and balances, and those who believe in a more efficient, autocratic, authoritarian system of government. And the failure of institutions during the previous administration has swung the pendulum toward authoritarianism.

*They are unable to understand that opposition is an integral part of how running a country works, and that those who disagree are just as much patriots as them, and simply see a different path out of the woods.*

To a certain extent I understand the supporters of Mr. Duterte. Most of them want the same things that I do: safe streets, trains that run on time, and a sense of sovereignty. They believe in the "Singapore model" of discipline, order, and hierarchical leadership. I could even come to an agreement with them on some points if only Mr. Duterte's administration were not one of such grinding stupidity, and his tactics so bullying, and his most outspoken supporters so vile. They are unable to understand that opposition is an integral part of how running a country works, and that those who disagree are just as much patriots as them, and simply see a different path out of the woods.

Instead of debate and dialogue, disagreement and dissent are dealt with using the tactics of the schoolground bully: threats, sometimes carried out, of physical harm, rape, murder. Online, they engage in the worst possible behavior, swarming the feeds and accounts of their dissenters with ad hominem attacks; they use lies and half-truths to fuel their arguments, and they are impervious to considering opposing views. "So what are you going to do about it? Oh, are you going to cry? Go on, run to the Commission on Human Rights, run to the UN and hide behind their skirts."

But why would they act otherwise, when their hero employs these tactics himself and carries himself with sarcastic braggadocio and channels Hugo Chavez in his dealings with diplomats, when he lashes out at critics by calling out their personal lives. Worryingly, he has alienated the Philippines' biggest strategic ally, the United States, not just by insulting their president, but forgoing important bilateral talks in a childish sulk. He has also lashed out at the UN and the EU for daring to criticize the effectiveness and methods of his drug war.

*But why would they act otherwise, when their hero employs these tactics himself and carries himself with sarcastic braggadocio and channels Hugo Chavez in his dealings with diplomats, when he lashes out at critics by calling out their personal lives.*

In every conflict it is worth looking for the humanity in one's adversaries, and I would like to think that most of Mr. Duterte's supporters are people who have the country's best interests at heart, but see a different, darker, harsher form of government than the one I want. At the far end of the spectrum are the trolls and extremists, rumored to be paid to use social media to attack, but perhaps—and I'm honestly not sure which is worse—not paid, and simply hateful people dripping with vitriol and willing to stoop to the lowest depths of dirty trickery and foul language to keep dissenters in line. At the moment there is simply no communication going on between the factions of those who support the president and his administration, and those who are critical of it. To even dare raise objections gets one labeled as an "enemy of change," and are punished by online shaming and harassment—and they are no less hurtful for being online.

For those who support the president and his methods, I must ask: Where is your moral compass? Where is your basic sense of decency and humanity? Do you believe that the end justifies the means? Because if so then I have news for you: This is not the story arc of a television show. There is no end in politics: it goes on and on and turns into history. The various means available to do things: the way we build a society, the way we disagree, the way we choose to solve problems; these are all we have.

*He is a bully and a narcissist; he has no regard for human life and basic morality; his obsession with the war on drugs precludes his involvement in other pressing internal and external matters that bore him and will be delegated to the incompetent or the corrupt; and he brings out the worst in both his supporters and his detractors. He is simply the wrong man for the job, and even his most fanatic devotees should pause for a moment and check in with their humanity at the most basic level.*

Those of us who believe that government should be run as a set of institutions that collide because they must, and impose checks and balances against one another can very well see the merits of the opposing point of view that a single strong leader with a compliant government could work in certain circumstances, with the right person.

But Mr. Duterte is not that person. Even as he reaches his first 100 days, this is patently obvious. He is a bully and a narcissist; he has no regard for human life and basic morality; his obsession with the war on drugs precludes his involvement in other pressing internal and external matters that bore him and will be delegated to the incompetent or the corrupt; and he brings out the worst in both his supporters and his detractors. He is simply the wrong man for the job, and even his most fanatic devotees should pause for a moment and check in with their humanity at the most basic level.

Worryingly, while the outraged middle classes are busy being aghast at the incivility of it all, and fighting ideological battles about the Marcos burial, he has quietly been amassing more power for himself. His first executive order as president is a reorganization of the Executive Department that creates a narrow hierarchy with one of his closest aides at the top. He has proposed a tenfold increase in the budget of the Office of the President. He has also asked Congress to sign off on a fuller reorganization act of the various bureaux and departments of the government—an alarming proposition, given his alliances and intents. This has happened only four times in the past: 1935, 1946, 1972, and 1987; if you think about those dates closely you will understand the kind of sea change that is imminent. And not least of all, hovering over all of this, is his plan to move toward a federal and parliamentary system of government; again, I am open to the idea, but under different circumstances: this is not the right time, and this is not the right man.

*Worryingly, while the outraged middle classes are busy being aghast at the incivility of it all, and fighting ideological battles about the Marcos burial, he has quietly been amassing more power for himself.*

The popularity of the president and the willingness of his supporters to abandon common sense and openness to debate and dissent has become a magnet for a power play among the political elite that will change the landscape of Philippine politics for generations. The most obvious is, of course, the move toward a dictatorship; this will not be opposed by the majority of the politicians as long as they have a seat at the table. The ousting of Leila de Lima as justice committee chairperson in the Senate proves that Mr. Duterte and the oligarchic coalition behind him have the numbers for it.

More importantly, he has if not the support, then at least the consent, of the people. Through a clever use of propaganda, fake news, appeals to emotion, distortion of facts, and simply making things too confusing for people to follow and understand, there is popular support for authoriarian rule. It is amazing how quickly things have moved: we are just approaching the new president's first 100 days, and Dutertopia is already here. Was our democracy so weak, that it be so easily felled in one quick blow? Was our resentment at the elite so strong and so easily channeled? Are we so blind, so easily swayed by rhetoric of violence, so easily cowed, so quick to fall in line and obey?

*Through a clever use of propaganda, fake news, appeals to emotion, distortion of facts, and simply making things too confusing for people to follow and understand, there is popular support for authoritarian rule.*

How long, then, must we go on being outraged? How long before we act? We can take it lying down, or we can take it on our knees; either way, we'll be screwed, just in a different way. The only way not to be is to be on our feet and fighting;

but the opposition is scarce and scraggly, we don't have the numbers, and we don't have a leader behind whom we can rally. The safest recourse is to wait, and make feeble protests, the kind we make when someone else offers to pay for the bill.

But the safest option might not be the best one, and even as a despot shows his true colors he is less and less easily unseated. We will grow less safe, our government less democratic, our country less civil.

# 3.

## Dear Mr. President

*Originally published in <u>Sunstar Davao</u>.*
*Email me at <u>andy@freethinking.me</u>. View previous*
*articles at <u>www.freethinking.me</u>.*

(Photo Credit: <u>jjpacres</u> Flickr via <u>Compfight</u> <u>cc</u>)
Dateline: Election 2016

Many years ago, when my father was still alive (and perhaps the same age as you are now), we had a long talk — just me and him. I had decided to be open and honest to him about certain behaviors he was exhibiting that I found disturbing. So for perhaps the first time in my life, I decided to be quite candid about it. The conversation went better than I expected. He did not react in anger and in fact opened up to me about his struggles with the same problem I noticed. So I understood him better after that, and my respect for him was not diminished in any way.

So I write to you today, not as a critic nor a detractor, but as one of your supporters and as one of the people who voted for you. I write openly with no intention of pulling you down or of lambasting you in public, but with the intention of giving voice to my fellow supporters who feel the same way as me but cannot express what they feel in their hearts nor have a venue for doing so. I write to you as a son of Davao of which you have been a father for many years. I was born here in the 70's and grew up here in the 80's. I know what Davao was back then and I know what it is now.

I write to implore you of one thing and one thing only, and it is not even unique: Please choose your words carefully. Please learn to control yourself.

I understand that in the election season, your street language was what endeared you to your voters and also attracted media to you to provide the necessary exposure and mileage to win. However, it is no longer election time. You have already won and have just marked your first 100 days as president. You no longer need the media splash and attention yet you are still getting it, for all the wrong reasons.

I understand that you do not really care what other people say about you. I used to be that way until I learned that some things I said hurt people I deeply cared about, even if I had no intentions of doing so. Like you, I had to apologize and explain myself several times, and I knew I had to work on improving my behavior, because apologies and explanations can get old pretty fast and people will tire of it if they see no true intent to change.

Speaking of which, your whole campaign was built on this one word: change. You promised to bring change and indeed we have seen many changes for the better in this short time, yet they have been overshadowed by the same careless language that you used prior to assuming office. It is ironic that in this regard, you have been showing a seeming unwillingness to change — you give reasons like you are really just fit to be a mayor and that people should not mind your mouth or your words too much.

May I respectfully remind you, sir, that words have power — as I'm sure you understand when you use those words to instill fear in criminals. Words can heal and words can kill — they can inspire a person to dizzying heights, yet also bring him down to the depths of despair. However, the sword cuts both ways and the careless use of words can come back to bite you as well when they cause people to be unsure of what you are saying and to lose their respect for you.

Also, change starts with yourself. In fact, may I remind you of your promise to be more "presidentiable" once you are elected? We cheered your efforts to change that one time you caught yourself before uttering a curse in a televised interview, but you soon slipped back into your old ways. Change is most effective when it comes from within, when people start doing things because they are right, not just because they fear the consequences of doing wrong. As our leader, showing to us your sincerity and willingness to change for the better will go a long way in inspiring others to do so.

When asked to describe your first 100 days in one word, one of my acquaintances answered, "polarizing" and as much as it pains me to hear it, I have to admit it is also true. Your detractors from before the elections have not been won over and have in fact, entrenched themselves further from you. The moderates have swung to either unapologetically defending you or outright hating you.

Mr. President, Mr. Mayor, *Tatay*, whether you like it or not, you are now president of the country, not just your 16 million voters, but of 100 million

Filipinos. We are watching your every move and taking cues from every little thing you say and do. It is your unenviable task to bring us all together – red, white, blue and even yellow – not to let us drift further apart.

And it all begins with your words, for words shape our beliefs and beliefs inspire our actions. Imagine 100 million Filipinos with one mind, one vision and one goal. That would be a force that can change the world.

---oOo---

# 4.

## Please PAY ATTENTION
## Mr. Duterte!

**From: pazogie <pazogie2003@yahoo.com>**

Dateline: Sunday, October 30, 2016
(Published in several yahoogroups, where pazogie
is a member)

DU30 WILL NOT RELEASE THE 6,000 NAMES OF POLICEMEN INCLUDED IN HIS 3RD LIST OF SUSPECTS. HE IS NOT GOING TO SHAME THEM LIKE HE DID TO THOSE IN THE FIRST LIST AND TO SEN. DE LIMA. Ah, ehem... if he does, he fears a terrible thing will happen to him and his administration of CHILLING FEAR employed in his TERRORISM STRATEGY to get what he wants, not for his own people that he is slowing killing, but for himself, Russia and CHINA or whom? For China because he said, "Goldberg started it all!" Yes, chimes in his aides, Goldberg started the word war and they expect us to believe. TERRIFIC! While the killing continues, either by the police or who knows who they are.

Now what does Du30 intend to do to the suspects he named and shamed who has yet to be formally charged in court? Wait for more rehab money from China or is waiting for orders from Xi? When the courts finally declare a good many of them innocent, where will we find Du30 and his apology? Will he pay for the damages suffered by them from the "Shoot to Kill" NOW trigger happy fingers of his PNP operatives led by the loyal raving General Stone [who took pride when an Indonesian said to him that his country is interested in following his Drug War? Nagkukunwari pa na hindi alam na binibiro lang siya!]

The other day I heard Du20 saying again he will next go after the corrupt. I wonder what the CHINA strategy will be? I heard from USA Ambassador Goldberg that Sen. Cayetano and Tugade were in a publicized trip to China in June right after the election, most certainly for the purpose of asking for advice how China can help in Du30's administration. Hey, did Du30's first 100 days' blueprint come from China and not from the CIA? Remember China wrote the book, "Be the best corrupt and succeed!"

When Du30 finally goes against the grafters, will the arrested have a special jail because the present jails cannot even accommodate half of the suspected drug criminals? Besides, practically all of the 6.8M workers in the government services are corrupt in varying degrees, from the janitors to the highest officials. The 6,000 alleged policemen in the 3rd list will be a big special problem because they cannot be jailed together with the drug criminals already overfilling our prisons. I wonder if it was Xi who advised Du30 to keep the 6,000 PNP suspects [already transferred to other commands] out of the limelight?

Going against all the criminals in government is a gargantuan task that cannot be done in 6 years of the whole of Du30's term or life. The dictator Marcos tried in 20 years and he ended up with more corruption than when he started his ML. How will

Du30 end up after 6 years? Many who tried ended in failure at the expense of many innocent and guilty lives who were unjustly terminated.

Fighting corruption and illegal drugs are never a "killing" proposition with cardboard signs of "Huwag tularan ang ganitong kriminal." [Yet to be put around a dead president, opponents pray] Why? Because, first of all, corruption is already part of the culture of Filipinos. How does one go about curing a cultural defect? Marcos wanted to cut down by half the too long generations period for culture to change by starting with his "Hitler boys" and an end plan of making him a monarch complete with a family history of royal lineage [nakita daw po itong planong ito sa isang drawer sa Malacanang pagkaalis ni Marcos patungong Hawaii].

Corruption is a product of our culture and where did we get it? From the daily exposure of the run of Filipino life - social, political, economics and religious. If corruption is a product, then it is an effect and the cause is the defective culture. We understand that killing the effect is not killing the cause. Will someone tell Du30 about this truth? He already knows but...

Aspiring to be with the Joneses next door corrupts because to do so is to aspire to be rich and aspiring to be rich in a corrupt capitalist republic is to engage in corruption [testifies Trump, hahaha]. Aspiring to be employed corrupts, too. To become the best lawyer, prosecutor and judge is to undergo a trial of corruption that cannot be declined. Working in government institutions corrupts. Betting in legal and illegal gambling corrupts. Farming and fishing are now filled with corrupt practices - from acquiring fertilizers to selling substandard products.

Supervising and managing use corrupt practices. Employees engage in petty to the worst kind of corruption, alone or in groups. Religious rites - baptism, marriage, fiestas is tinged with corruption [including Sinulogs, fake Magellan spices voyage, fake Sto Nino icon, fake Battle of Mactan with no Lapulapu in a no "settlement to be found in Mactan then" corrupt, with lies of Pigafetta, etc.]. TV and the Internet corrupt - easily the young malleable minds. Foreign aids and loans corrupt - the China-Arroyo deals were telling examples. Working in financial institutions corrupts - like the recent bank scandal involving foreign nationals and our local bank with laundering Chinese partners engaged in cleaning dirty money in Casinos where Erap is mayor. Friars and guardia civils corrupted the poor Filipinos of Rizal's time...Rizal, he was too kind to mention government positions sold to a lot of land grabbers, corrupt friends and relatives. Gen. Howling Mad Genocide Smith and his soldiers used the corrupting tit for tat to sow fear for the White supremacists. Democracy and voting corrupt. Passports and licenses corrupt. Enforcement tasks corrupt...

Vending of any kind, legal or illegal, domestic or international corrupt... Corruption is in all over the Filipinos' life from birth to death. Bah, it is a part of the culture in every people. What a consuelo de bobo!

In one of our seminars with an ex-Ombudsman guest speaker in the early years of 2000, he revealed to us with a serious sad face that corruption is part of our culture. After he made the revelation all the participants, all government employees, suddenly became silent with a few wearing a wry smile. Some turned to face one another looking a bit annoyed, perhaps for having been uncovered but not surprised, and trying their best to hide a guilty look.

Where do we begin tracing when corruption started to take roots? From the days of early man as he hunted for food and cared for his family? Scarcity and competition introduce innocent man to corruption. Such a long way. But Du30 need not labor much on this tiring task. He admits he doesn't have time to learn, hehe, let China or the CIA take care of the studies and he will just implement their recommendations without understanding. And HOW!! With a lot of "excuses the president has to make that you, like us his close aides, cannot fathom because we don't know him very well yet. We have to give ourselves time to understand what he means that he is just aping most of the time in accordance to his Manual of Operations that he didn't write. Please give him time to learn the tricks a decent and respectable president have to study, er. just follow with, dear me, no ad libs."

I am for helping anyone who is frank and honest with me, but who in this world is the Lord and Master who is ever frank and honest to a lowly citizen like me? I am not one to follow anyone who says, "I, your president of 102M people elected by 16M voters orders you, Ogie, to be with me in our country's trip to success with China and Russia.. fuck the USA!" I like the president of a democratic republic to seek his people's true sentiments [from surveys???] and not one who pretends to listen but do not hear.

At the end of a consultative session, as his close aides have been saying, he follows his own inner voice. But NOW ALL OF A SUDDEN, he claims with a clown's amusing face of following orders by obeying the Book, WITH GOD directly TALKING TO HIM!

What a bull-shitter this anti-Pope is! He never understood and followed God's "Thou shall not take the Lord thy God in vain." So, he curses God's rep, the Pope, and tells the people, God spoke to me to stop my cursing otherwise he will make his plane crash!" He, he, he also is deaf to the command, "Thou shall not kill" [with no due process!]. He-he-he to tell the people he suddenly heard, listened, and intent to heed God's killing warning if he does not stop swearing is to fuck the people. He is trying to con the people again with another big lie so he can be a respected leader of the 95% God fearing constituency whom he promised to kill 1.8M of them if given the opportunity. Too bad for them, now he has the opportunity. Too bad really, because God suddenly acknowledged by telling him directly that it is OK to warn suspects and kill them if they disobey. Gosh, God and Du30, birds of the same feather, are thinking and doing the same things. Er, it is just his way of looking at God , a killing God that according to Poch is nothing new. In fact, it is in the Bible.

I don't know what is going to happen to us with Du30. He didn't do a fine start by his passion for vengeance, to insult people and abuse his new found powers to shame and kill without due process. I hope he will improve and do well along the way. It is a very serious hope even as he tries to make me laugh with his fake "juvenile" innocence in the field of diplomacy and standard right conduct. And with his "new" Godliness ploy. Excuse me.

Psst...Sorry, if I appear ranting, Danny. But if I am, Du30 has my excuse - "I am new in this job but rest assured what I say comes from deep in my heart."

Oh, I meant to ask you, did his 16M voters heard him and agreed with him during the campaign that they will welcome the communism of China to replace our democracy? If not, he is now dictating to them what they want him to do.

WOW what a fine show of leadership! Boy, we have lots to learn from this guy, particularly in the area of good governance with easy lies and shallow excuses, and ethical standards of behavior at home, abroad and with our guests.

Enshrined in our laws is this principle, "Assumption of public office is impressed with the paramount public interest that requires the highest standards of ethical conduct." I believe the improper conduct of cursing and disrespect he has shown is an impeachable offense. "Putang Ina Mo" [like mother fucker] is becoming a standard ethical invective among the young who think that if our president can do it without bad consequences to him, particularly to foreign dignitaries, they can do it, too. They are impressed by his misplaced "tough curses" and disregard for established tradition, time honored ways of respecting each other. Why not? He has not been punished for doing it. Soooo, it is ok for them, they who learn best by catching acted-words than being taught in school by mere abstract words.

All the best,
Ogie

---oOo---

# 5.

# A Dark Night at the Well (fiction) by Fred Natividad

Dateline: November 2, 2016
<frednati@yahoo.com>

It is not yet nine o'clock but it is already very dark. The sacristan's helper has not rung the church bell yet to remind parishioners to do their nine o'clock evening prayers. There is neither a moon nor are there electric streetlights, as the whole town of Apangat will not have electricity until some years later. Because of darkness the evening seems deeper into the night than it actually is.

Indong is about to go to sleep when his mother discovers that the water jar in the kitchen are empty. It is one of Indong's chores (on top of taking care of three goats) to see to it that there is always water in the jars for drinking and cooking. It is not usual for him to fetch water on a dark night but he has to do it this time so he will be free early next morning. He has to go to school early to join a class excursion and he has to do the breakfast cooking as ordered by his mother.

So Indong goes to the well, silently grumbling, shouldering a hollowed out bamboo tube as his vessel to carry water. It is dark at the well but he felt confidently able that he can connect the open end of his bamboo tube to the faucet due to the countless times that he had fetched water there. But because it is dark he did not immediately realize that somebody is bathing in a huddled position under the waist-high faucet of the free-flowing well.

"Hey, I am here, please wait a little bit," he hears a woman's voice.

He is startled but it does not take long for his eyes to adjust in the darkness to see a naked woman huddled under the free flowing faucet. She turns out to be Manang Elena. She covers herself with her arms when she hears Indong approaching. It is a futile effort because there is not much that two arms can do to cover one's naked body. When she recognizes Indong she lets her guard down and lets her hands fall down limply, uncovering herself. She knows him as one of her younger brother's playmates, just a ten-year old kid still sexually innocent and harmless. She feels no need to hide herself from him.

Her house is just across the street from the well. Indong has heard from older boys that it is not unusual for her to take baths at the well on dark nights when it is supposedly already late enough that nobody would come to fetch water anymore. They love to tell stories at how, from a discreet distance behind an acacia tree, they lasciviously enjoy peeping at her.

On some nights in the hot summer the older boys take baths naked in the dark, too, just to cool off. Because they make a lot of noise, those are nights that Elena does not dare to bathe herself.

There is one night when the boys, while carousing naked at the well, thought of serenading Elena in the buff as a prank. Serenading girls is a traditional pastime of young men in Apangat, especially when a girl from out of town would visit to spend the night with relatives and this night Elena's cousin came to visit. The boys cross the street without their clothes and sneak quietly beneath the window of Elena's room. Someone begins to pluck introductory notes on the guitar and the designated serenader begins to belt out a tender, traditional old ballad imploring a maiden to please pity a forlorn lover by opening her window and all that mushy stuff.

Elena does open her window just a little crack so she could peer down at the serenaders. She takes turns peering down in the dark with her visiting cousin and they both agree that the serenaders are probably men from the local Constabulary detachment out for an evening of relaxation. Maybe the group is led by Elena's long time suitor, a Philippine Constabulary officer. In the dark the men appear to be wearing khakis due to their naked brownness. The girls innocently strike a match to light a kerosene lamp and when they open the window wider to peer down with the lamp the naked boys below scatter in all directions!

Indong remembers that story as he gets closer to Elena. In the dark her nakedness is not totally clear. From this he discovers that the older boys just told tall tales when they describe her nakedness. They had to be some distance away so as not to spook her so they could not have seen her clearly in the dark.

Elena, nineteen years old, is quite pretty. But from Indong's ten-year old perspective she is an old maid. Gossiping busybodies had established that she was forever refusing to get involved with the Philippine Constabulary officer who comes to woo her only about once a month because he is always getting assigned to missions all over the central plains.

She refused to marry him because she is afraid to wind up becoming his widow. At that time the Philippine Constabulary was always suffering casualties fighting bandits or communists called Huks, or Muslims called Moros who violently protest Christian encroachment of their ancestral lands.

"Oops, I am sorry, Manang Elena," Indong apologizes when he accidentally touched her naked back while groping in the dark trying to connect the open end of his bamboo tube to the faucet. Elena's kid brother addresses her "Manang" - big sister - in deference to her being his big sister. So, with the same deference Indong also addresses her as Manang Elena.

"It's okay, Indong," she said. "Here," she hands him a fragrant bath soap, "please soap the part of my back that I can't reach."

Because he wants to get home fast it bothers him that he has to be delayed lathering somebody's back. But he puts aside his bamboo tube. While he lathers her, his eyes adjust further in the dark. He works from her right side and since her body is lighter than the blackness of the night he has an opaque dim side view of her.

When he is done he attempts to give the now slippery soap to her but it falls off his hands. He quickly tries to retrieve it only to brush his hands against her front. She does not seem disturbed. After all he is only a ten-year old boy.

"Okay, I got it," she says as she picks up the soap and begins lathering the front of her body. It silently irritates him further that he has to wait her soap and rinse herself before he could fill up his bamboo tube and go home.

In the days that follow after that night he begins to take notice of girls for the first time in his growing years. Every time he sees Elena he feels he could see underneath her blouse. He remembers that in the darkness he could see the blurred contour of her nakedness.

One time he wakes up with a start, frightened, in the middle of the night. He had a weird dream of doing something taboo. He dreamed making love in broad daylight to a beautiful grown woman at the well while older boys heckled and laughed at his clumsiness. It is when he finds himself staring at the woman's face staring back from under him that he wakes up with a frightening jolt.

The beautiful but very angry face of Manang Elena stares at him with eyes that spurts red-hot fire. Then she becomes a man with the angry face of a constabulary officer. He gets up from the bed to find himself breathing heavily with his shirt wet with perspiration.

He realizes he is now a young man, no longer a ten-year old unaware of girls.

---ooo---

# 6.

## Duterte's Flip-Flop Diplomacy

### Perry Diaz
Dateline: November 2, 2016 - PerryScope

When President Rodrigo "Digong" Duterte announced his "separation" from the United States during his state visit to China, it shook the world. Not that it would have changed the balance of power in the Indo-Asia-Pacific region, but it was because of the abrupt – "strange," I might say – way of which it was announced. But what is surreally baffling is his retraction the next day. Is it a case of Dr. Jekyll and Mr. Hyde syndrome or it's just plain grandstanding?

One personality wants to maintain the status quo on U.S.-Philippine relations while the other personality wants to sever all ties with the U.S. and align with the "ideological flow" of China and Russia. And in a moment of Napoleonic illusion, he saw himself as part of an alliance – China, Philippines, and Russia — against the world! Why didn't he include North Korea?

The problem is: Duterte (also known as Du30) seems to live in his own little world totally detached from the geopolitical realities that dictate how nations – and their leaders — interact with one another. He seems to think of the Philippines as an island onto itself that can provide security for her people without help from anybody. And, worst, dismantling the Philippines' military ties with the U.S. would strip the Philippines of the capability to defend her sovereignty and territorial integrity.

**Digong's brand of geopolitics**

**Duterte, Xi, and Putin.**

Evidently, Duterte's brand of geopolitics digresses from established norms and conventions in international relations. His handling of the Philippines' West Philippine Sea/South China Sea claims vis-à-vis the Permanent Court of Arbitration's (PCA) ruling, which is overwhelmingly favorable to the Philippines, has bungled the country's strong case against China. Had Duterte stayed on course in pursuing the Philippines' claims, the other claimant-countries could have used the PCA ruling to pursue their own maritime claims against China.

It's interesting to note that with all the geopolitical mishaps and diplomatic faux pas that Duterte did, he had the temerity to claim that he was a Foreign Service graduate. At a press conference last October 19 during his state visit to China,

Filipino journalist Ellen Tordesillas quoted him in her column as saying: *"Now that I am the President, by the grace of God, I read a lot; I'm a lawyer and I studied geopolitics and all, and also I am a graduate of the Foreign Service so I get to know how to balance this contending (forces)."*

But what Digong did was break one of the rules of geopolitics, which is: *"Geopolitics is not a zero-sum game."* Indeed, in today's globalized economy, the object of geopolitics is to arrive at a win-win situation where players need to compromise. Gone are the days when nations go to war to settle territorial disputes. The Cold War is over and we are now living in a multipolar world order where all nations are interdependent with one another. The world is shrinking too; and everybody is just a "click" away.

*Philippine President Rodrigo Duterte, center, accompanied by Transportation Secretary Arthur Tugade, right, and Defense Secretary Delfin Lorenzana, left, clap their hands at the end of Japan's coast guard drills in Yokohama, Oct. 27, 2016.*

Digong's attempted maneuver to "separate" from the U.S. — militarily and economically — and threatened to form an alliance with China and Russia, did not only fail to materialize but it also made a "village clown" of himself. And while he made all these geopolitical and diplomatic boo-

boos, his Foreign Secretary Perfecto Yasay Jr. and Defense Secretary Delfin Lorenzana had the thankless job of straightening out the knots and kinks of his "independent foreign policy," which has been causing a lot of embarrassment for him.

**It's all drama**

With all the "Du30 drama" he staged in Beijing, Duterte was able to attract $24 billion in investments and loans from China. It must have made Chinese President Xi Jinping feel triumphant that the Philippines — under Duterte's leadership – is now in his pocket, totally detached from the U.S. And it would certainly have given him a firm grip on the vast South China Sea. Wrong!

The day Digong returned to the Philippines, he clarified that he's not cutting ties with the U.S. He said he was just pursuing a "separation of foreign policy" from the U.S., which was quite different in meaning and purpose to what he proclaimed in China, which was "separation from the U.S." He said that he didn't want it to affect local jobs in American-owned companies in the Philippines and the large number of Filipinos in the U.S. He also said that it is in the best interest of the Philippines to maintain diplomatic relations with the U.S.

**Volte face**

An article on the *Nikkei Asian Review* titled, ***"Duterte's 'about-face' unsettles***

*Xi,"* published last October 28, talked about Duterte's *volte face* [an act of turning around so as to face in the opposite direction] upon his return to the Philippines. The report said: *"The Internet was not slow to react to Duterte's volte face, and the word 'fraud' has gone viral. One social media post read, 'Duterte changed his face as soon as he returned to the Philippines after securing money from China.'*

*"The reference was to the traditional Chinese art of 'face changing,' where performers go from one character to the next by swapping masks in a Beijing opera or during a banquet. Many feel it was not the mask that was changed so much as a complete change of heart.*

*"Other online posts put it in less uncertain terms, 'China got dumped. China was deceived,' read one. Another said, 'It is a divorce in disguise [from the U.S.] for the sake of borrowing [from China]. That's not uncommon in China.' "*

### Damage control

*Foreign Secretary Perfecto Yasay Jr. informed Romualdez of his appointment yesterday at the Imperial Tower Hotel in Tokyo, on the sidelines of Duterte's three-day official visit.*

It must have occurred to Duterte that he didn't have to let go of the U.S. now that he had secured a huge economic package from China. During his subsequent visit to Japan following the China trip, he appointed *Philippine Star* columnist Babe Romualdez as special envoy to the U.S., reportedly as part of a "rebooting" of relationship with the U.S.

The *Philippine Star* report said: *"Foreign Secretary Perfecto Yasay Jr. informed Romualdez of his appointment yesterday at the Imperial Tower Hotel in Tokyo, on the sidelines of Duterte's three-day official visit.*

*" 'We are trying on how we can work with the changes… especially with the upcoming elections in the US so we will see how we can (establish)… let's call it as rebooting our relationship with the US,' said a member of the President's official delegation here.*

*" 'We'd like to communicate the message of how we will have a rebooting of our relationship,' the official, who declined to be named, added. 'Yes, of course we will continue our relationship with the US.'*

*"As special envoy, Romualdez's 'special mission' is to put back on track Philippine-US relations,"* the report concluded, which begs the question: Can Romualdez fix the damage Digong made?

### Geopolitics is addition

*Duterte and U.S. Secretary of State John Kerry.*

Now that Digong has his cake, he wants to eat it, too. But while a zero-sum game might produce intermediate success in the short term, just like what Digong did on his China visit; he should – nay, must! — realize that in the long term, good geopolitics produces better results if it weren't played as a zero-sum game. It reminds me of the late legendary political leader Eulogio "Amang" Rodriguez whose mantra was "Politics is addition." And so is Geopolitics.

At the end of the day, Digong's flip-flop diplomacy may have worked in his favor at this time, but he must be careful because it could boomerang the next time he flip-flops.

---ooo---

# 7.

## Did China Trick Digong?
### Perry Diaz

**Dateline. Nov. 7, 2016, PerryScope**

When President Rodrigo "Digong" Duterte was sworn in last June 30, 2016, the first person he introduced to the audience was former President Fidel V. Ramos, whom he credited for helping him launch his presidential candidacy. It did not then come as a surprise when Digong appointed Ramos as his special envoy to China.

Immediately, Ramos went to Hong Kong to make contact with a former high-ranking Chinese official and a few other Chinese personalities to "break the ice." But as Ramos had told reporters upon his return to Manila, "It's not really a breakthrough in a sense that there is no ice here in Hong Kong to break but the fish we eat... are cooked in delicious recipes."

After that, Duterte's people started making arrangements for his China trip. They even had a date set for the visit – October 18-21. But the official invitation did not come until the last minute. With an entourage of more than 400 business people, cabinet members, presidential aides, generals, journalists, and kibitzers, Digong flew into the red dragon's lair. After four days of bad-mouthing the Americans, he brought home $24 billion in investment pledges and loans, including $13.5 billion in trade deals. The question is: what concession did he give the Chinese?

But no sooner had Digong landed in Manila than he pivoted 180 degrees and reaffirmed U.S.-Philippine ties. Given his avowed dislike – or to be more precise, hatred of the U.S. – why would he make a fool of himself with such diplomatic boo-boos and flip-flops? Or, as Americans love to say, "Are you out of your mind?"`

**Dangerous game**

Well, Duterte is not out of his mind but what appeared to have happened was he was playing China and the U.S. off each other, perhaps hoping to get the best of both worlds. But what he didn't realize was that he was dealing with pros. China is the second biggest economic power next to the U.S.

and for a third-world country to play China against the U.S. – the Philippines' treaty ally – is something that's not in the playbook of geopolitics. Nobody has done that and succeeded in getting concessions from both sides. On the contrary, Digong might find himself caught in a vise because China and the U.S. are big trading partners with interlocking economic interests. So, when push comes to shove, the two superpowers could – or would –find ways to amicably settle their differences and throw Digong under the bus.

### What China wants

### Nine-dash line

But ultimately, China would try to get what she had always wanted – sovereignty over the South China Sea (SCS), which includes all the islands, rocks, reefs, and shoals in these waters. And also all the marine resources, and oil and gas deposits, which would provide China with food and energy for her 1.4 billion people. Thus, there is just no way that China would give away any part of the SCS without going to war, which Duterte already conceded when he said, "We cannot win a war with China." However, Senior Associate Justice Antonio Carpio said at the closing ceremony of the 33rd Philippines-U.S. Amphibious Landing Exercise (Phiblex) last October 12, "There is only one power on earth that can stop the Chinese and that's the U.S." Digong knows that. And the Chinese know it, too. They also know that the Philippines a geostrategic buffer zone that the U.S. can use to counter China and prevent her from breaking out into the Second Island Chain in the Western Pacific, America's last line of defense.

With five Philippine military bases that the Americans can use to deploy their forces, it would be too much of a risk for China to start a war in the SCS. However, if war breaks out, the Philippines will be on the front-line, which is just around 100 miles from the Spratly archipelago where China had built seven militarized artificial islands. Then there are the U.S. bases in Japan, South Korea, Australia, and Singapore. And with five aircraft carrier battle groups under the joint command of the 3rd Fleet and 7th Fleet and a fleet of nuclear ballistic missile submarines, the U.S. would have more than sufficient forces to maintain peace and stability in the Indo-Asia-Pacific Region… and keep China at bay.

### Quid pro quo

*President Duterte cozying up to Chinese Ambassador to the Philippines Zhao Jianhua.*

Although Ramos was credited for "breaking the ice" in China-Philippine relations, what really paved the way for Digong's celebrated state visit to

China were Sen. Alan Peter Cayetano and Transportation Secretary Arthur Tugade's "unpublicized" – or secret – trip to China last June prior to Duterte's inauguration. U.S. Ambassador Philip Goldberg revealed this when he was recently interviewed at the ANC talk show, "Headstart." The question is: Did Cayetano and Tugade strike a "quid pro quo" deal with the Chinese?

Someone who may have played a key role in forging the Chinese-Philippine connection was Chinese Ambassador to the Philippines Zhao Jianhua. The groundwork for this "connection" may have been laid out when Zhao and several Chinese businessmen visited then president-elect Duterte in Davao City. Zhao, who had kept a low profile during former President Aquino's time, has been a "frequent visitor" to Davao City and Malacanang, conspicuously attired in a silk Kung Fu suit. He's often pictured with Duterte or Secretary of Foreign Affairs Perfecto Yasay Jr., the two people that matter most to him to advance China's interests. And if you look at what transpired in the first four months of Digong's presidency, Zhao was pretty darn successful.

**Red flags**

*Former Philippine President Fidel Ramos gestures as he speaks to journalists during a trip to Hong Kong, China after the Hague court's ruling over the maritime dispute in South China Sea, August 9, 2016. REUTERS/Tyrone Siu*

Ramos must have sensed that something was afoot after his ice-breaking "unofficial" trip to Hong Kong. He seems to have been sidelined by Duterte's "kitchen cabinet," which is presumably pro-China. About two weeks prior to Digong's China trip, Yasay informed Ramos that his trip to Beijing was cancelled. No reason was given for the cancellation; however, the speculation was that Ramos was an "Amboy" (American Boy), a pejorative for someone who is staunchly pro-American.

A few days before Duterte's China trip, Ramos informed Malacanang that he would not be part of the president's delegation. Communications Secretary Martin Andanar said in a press briefing, "He did not say why he won't join but I believe that it is about giving respect to our current President Rodrigo Duterte." But what else could he have said?

A week after Digong arrived from his China trip, Ramos resigned as special envoy to China. But for whatever official reasons why Ramos quit, it will surprise no one if the real reason for his resignation is that Duterte has become "toxic" – that is, politically hazardous — and has to dissociate and distance himself from him. Ramos, a West Point graduate, a retired Lt. General, hero of the EDSA People Power Revolution, and former president of the Philippines, is undoubtedly pro-American and anti-communist, which would certainly make China's leaders uneasy in dealing with him.

In an article reported in the Asia Times titled, "Has the Philippines blown its South China Sea win?" (November 2, 2016), it said: "The price the archipelago nation has paid — or will pay — for his

China pivot is also enormous. Besides economic and military separation from America, the Philippines' long-standing and most important ally, which will likely negatively impact his country in the long-term, if it is materialized, he has made substantial maritime and territorial concessions.

"With such lavish deals agreed with China, coupled with Beijing's claim of its inherent and indisputable sovereignty over most of the South China Sea, its opposition to the arbitration case and Duterte's alienation of the Philippines' key international partners and allies, the prospect that China will comply fully or even partly with the ruling has become unthinkable."

And this raises the question: Did China trick Digong into giving up so much for so little in return? It seems like it.

---oOo---

# 8.

# In Blackest Day and Darkest Night

## Jonathan Edwards J. Olabre
### Dateline: Nov. 9, 2016

The Supreme Court Decision of 9-5 junking the petition against the burial of former President Ferdinand E. Marcos at the Libingan ng mga Bayani came as a shock to those who expected a ruling favoring the petition. Indignation was instantaneous and spontaneous. By late afternoon, demonstrations and rallies were being undertaken in various locations.

For me, I was born in 1965. It took a while for all of it to sink in. Although I was distraught because the decision, a certain paralysis overtook me a few hours later. I felt anger at first, I refused to post anything on my Facebook account, limiting myself to commenting on posts made by friends. I tried to make sense of it, trying to find that silver lining. I even tried to look at it as perhaps a sign from God.

At my age now, I have already thought of my "escape plan". That is a contingency plan when I eventually will retire. It was a plan to leave everything behind. Having read so many books on how to secure the retirement years and not be dependent on pensions. Yesterday, it seemed that I better have another plan.

I only have to look at the faces of my nieces and nephews in my mind's eye. I could never in my life leave them to what has just transpired. Even just after the elections, my siblings who had children would talk and say that everything they had worked for and sacrificed for the future came crashing down. They said that "Nai-panalo na naming dati ang kalayaan (We have already won freedom before)." Why should our children live in fear 30 years after?

As I was in those thoughts, it again drifted further back. It was a time that there was no TV, or radio or newspapers came out. I was still in Grade 1 then. But almost immediately I felt the change. We had no classes for 1 month. Then before going to school, my elders told me not to talk about Marcos. I come from a politically active family and I had a grand uncle who was a senator at that time. We always opposed Marcos.

I learned about the curfew, whenever I see the Metrocom patrol car coming down the street, it was time to go inside the compound gate. I worried about watching my mouth in school. After Lupang Hinirang we were made to sing The Bagong Lipunan March every day. Our Social Studies subject was changed into reading and studying Junior Citizen and Current Events Digest whose main contents were the projects and programs of the New Society. We never learned about Bonifacio, Rizal, Mabini, etc.

But etched in my mind forever is the "Sona" done to our neighborhood. When the Metrocom and PC would conduct saturation drives. All men would be told to come out into the street, take off their clothes and be subjected to searched. The Metrocom carried a list wherein names were announced and those who were in the list were carried off. I peeked in one of our Capiz windows which I bored a hole to watch from inside.

For a child, such memories of terror would never be erased. My terror is still inside my head even up to now. I knew it was wrong and dangerous to fight against the regime, but I also was able to put my licks in. In 1978, when the Noise Barrage was being organized, the only way to convey the messages was by passing a piece of paper with instructions. I rode my bicycle past the Metrocom and PC checkpoints to pass along the message. I just graduated Grade 6 then. I remember the scenes so vividly util now and they were made even more vivid with the SC decision yesterday. It is like a recurring nightmare and Freddy Kreuger just keeps on returning.

The terror of yesteryears are creeping back. The SC just made all the terror justified by its ruling. The person who enveloped the country in darkness decades ago was rewarded for the act. His family is rejoicing and basking in their regained legitimacy.

There is anger, indignation and gnashing of teeth by those who survived and fought the dictatorship. I was talking to a friend, she just told me "Wala naman tayong magagawa (We cannot do anything)". A pall has descended over this benighted land.

The sacrifices made years before seem to have been made in vain. It is easy now to just accept what has befallen our land and our people. But the memories that were rekindled yesterday would never permit me to just roll over and die. In fact, it has reactivated long dormant fires that were just embers the day before.

My face and those faces of my friends are now interspersed with the faces of my nieces and nephews. Now I understand. It was never for us, the torch we carry is for them. This time around, the light will not be so easily snuffed out.

We owe it to our heroes, martyrs and sacred dead. In this Darkest Day and Blackest night.We will not fail them.

---oOo---

# 9.

## Yolanda 3rd Anniversary

### Enrico San Juan
Dateline: Nov 9, 2016

The commemoration of the 3rd anniversary of the super typhoon Yolanda's devastation in the Visayas was once again marred with the shortcomings of the previous administration. Funds were allegedly missing because the victims of the calamity are still suffering from poor living conditions.

Organizations under the auspices of the United Nations kept saying that our country is one of the vulnerable nations that has and will greatly suffer due to climate change. May it be dry or wet season, we experienced a great loss of lives and properties because of the so-called climate change (a.k.a. global warming).

Actually this could be the reason why the former president Fidel Ramos got pissed off when President Rody Duterte reiterated his stand against the signing of the Paris Agreement on Climate Change. It was in July that PDU30 hinted in his speech that he will not honor the climate change pact on carbon emission.

But last November 7, during a speech at the oath-taking of the new officers of the National Press Club in Malacañang Palace, the president announced his decision that he will now back the Paris Agreement on Climate Change, after a near-unanimous approval by his Cabinet, and he will be signing the historic pact.

According to the 2016 Climate Change Vulnerability Index, the Philippines is one of the 15 countries most vulnerable to climate change. But what is the Paris Agreement all about?

According to the article of Tony La Viña (former dean of the Ateneo School of Government) @rappler.com, "The Paris Agreement is not just a carbon emissions agreement but a comprehensive sustainable development agreement. It is an adaptation, loss and damage, finance, technology and capacity building agreement – all of which are essential to our survival. We cannot cherry-pick but have to accept the whole package. But we can do so in our own terms.

To opt out of the Paris Agreement is to allow developed countries to escape from their responsibility to compensate us for causing climate change. The Paris Agreement is the only process where we can get developed countries to be accountable for their emissions through a loss and damage mechanism and through provisions that require them as a matter of climate justice to provide support to us so we can adapt to and mitigate climate change. Indeed, the Paris Agreement has good provisions on finance, technology transfer, and capacity building. Our delegation worked hard in Paris to get the best text possible for these provisions.

The Paris Agreement does not impose emissions reduction limitations on us. We can determine our own targets based on our development needs. We can adopt targets but we can make that conditional on support by developed countries. That's what we did in Paris – we did offer 70% but we said we will do it only if support was given. If the Duterte administration wishes, it can lower the number to maybe 30-40% and perhaps commit to do 10-15% of that as unconditional since we are already doing many things on our own. Such a decision would be credible and acceptable.

The Paris Agreement is a good document whose consequences will last generations. While this legally binding agreement in itself is not enough to solve the climate crisis, it is as strong, ambitious, and as equitable as it can be for an agreement that required consensus by 195 countries—a positive beginning to a long and hard journey towards climate justice."

Yes, there are concerted efforts of countries around the world to address the so called threats of global warming/climate change but as what we have been saying for several years now in our radio program and in our writings that there is one element that this body is missing or has refused to acknowledge, which is the man-made cause of climate change, that is weather manipulation or weather engineering.

Strange behavior of weather systems and abnormal movements of typhoons that we have never before witnessed are the signatures of someone or something is really manipulating Mother Nature that has caused great dangers to humankind.

Could it be that through this evil science of manipulating weather is the reason for people of various nations to be compelled to sign a pact to address the man-made disaster? In the various UN-sponsored gatherings of leaders of various nations, there is always opposition to such move because it will only hamper the growth and development of countries especially the developing ones.

Treaties that will only manipulate nations and like a herd of cattle, will lead them to the slaughterhouse because the real culprit of such world disaster such as global warming is actually known as man-made and it will go on as long as the evil geniuses behind it are not exposed and punish.

Who may taught that such weather engineering is only seen in the sci-fi movies?

---oOo---

# 10.

## Memo to: The University Community Ateneo De Manila University

## Subject: Marcos burial issue

From: <u>Office of Alumni Relations</u>
Sent: Thursday, November 10, 2016 9:15 AM
To: <u>Worldwide 11-09-16</u>

**A MUST READ FOR ALL ! PLEASE PASS ON TO EVERYONE IN YOUR DIRECTORY.**

On 8 November 2016, the Supreme Court of the Republic of the Philippines decided to allow the burial of Dictator Ferdinand Marcos at the historic and symbolic Libingan ng mga Bayani. With no hesitation, the Ateneo de Manila University expresses its indignation over this decision, calling this an act of convenient equivocation and injustice on the part of the Supreme Court.

In its decision, the Supreme Court argued by saying: "While he was not all good, he was not pure evil either. Certainly, just a human who erred like us." Such an argument amounts to a monumental denial of the suffering and murder of thousands of our people and the billions of public funds stolen during those tragic years of Martial Law. Ferdinand Marcos did not just err like us. Decisions that were made during his regime were marked by atrocity and impunity. People were imprisoned, tortured, and killed just for harboring different beliefs and convictions. Those years were deliberately disruptive of democracy and freedom. Martial Law wasn't just a stumble in the dark. It was a careful orchestration of violence and power conducted in the name of order and an artificial peace.

The Supreme Court hides behind the letter of the law, taking the myopic view that the issue is one of mere legality and politics. The Court has chosen to pass this issue back on to the executive. In so doing, it misses the opportunity and its own power to affirm the enshrined principles embedded in our Constitution, which they have affirmed as rising from the ashes of the Marcos administration.

I call upon our community to continue to protest and express our indignation, to discern what true closure might mean concretely in this case, to create openings for our voice to be heard authentically, to protect the democratic space and engage in meaningful dialogue with our fellow Filipinos. It is easy to think of the other as enemy but we will not yield to the sinister forces that want to divide us now as a people. The only way to get to the true path of peace, justice and reconciliation is to engage in the process of listening to each other.

Even as we embark on these, I would like to remind everyone that not all wars are won on one battlefield. We will fight for the truth in our classrooms, in the work that we do in the communities we serve, in the many places in government, business, and civil society, wherever we find our alumni engaged in building our nation and our people, so that we will never forget what cannot and should not be forgotten.

In all these, we draw strength from the power of the cross of Christ, who calls us to stand in solidarity with those who incarnate his truth and love and justice.

amdg,
Jose Ramon T Villarin SJ
President

---oOo---

# 11.

# De La Salle Philippines Message: Marcos Burial – Never Forget

**Dateline: Nov 10, 2016**
**(Posted by: "Rey Fuentes")**

Lasallian Mission at DLSULike Page15, De La Salle Philippines (DLSP) Statement on the Supreme Court Decision on the Marcos' Burial-- Never Forget!

There can be no moving on without an accounting of the past, no forgiveness without remorse and apology. There can be no justice without accountability. There can be no justice with impunity. We are thus deeply despondent over the Supreme Court's (SC) failure to stand on what is just by affirming Ferdinand Marcos' planned burial at the Libingan ng mga Bayani (LNMB). The Court, on the petition against the President's order for the burial of Marcos' remains in the LNMB, has sadly chosen to err on the side of technicality rather than that of history.Marcos is not a hero. He was an oppressive ruler and a dictator. The empowering experience and triumph of all freedom-loving Filipinos over authoritarianism through People Power 1 in February 1986 is a clear rejection of the Marcos regime. He remains answerable for many counts of atrocities and human rights violations as well as ill-gotten wealth.

The SC decision, an ominous development, reflects the weakness of our democracy to exact accountability from leaders who abused and are abusing their power. Unfortunately, after EDSA People Power 1, the task of deepening and consolidating our democracy by strengthening our institutions, including the courts, has not been assiduously pursued. The same weakness has now been taken advantage of by the Marcos family. This challenges our schools all the more, to help clarify for and with younger generations and those who engage us, the lessons borne out of a scrupulous study of history, citizenship, accountability, and good governance.

We therefore call on all our Lasallian teachers and partners to strengthen all their educational and community engagement efforts and programs towards a deepening of our people's appreciation for democracy and human rights. Let us join with like-minded groups to create more robust advocacy on these issues. Let us oppose every effort to distort our nation's story. We shall endeavor to re-tell our story so that we remain true to the values we have fought for and for which many have given up their lives.

The oppressiveness of Marcos' Martial Law must not be forgotten. NEVER AGAIN!Br. Jose Mari L. Jimenez FSC President, De La Salle Philippines (DLSP) 10 November 2016

---oOo---

# 12.

## An Open Letter To Donald Trump, My Former Boss Of 18 Years

### (I know you can  be a good president. Good luck.)

**By Barbara Res**
<http://www.huffingtonpost.com/author/ barbara-res>Engineer,
**Attorney, Mediator, Author Construction Manager**
Dateline, 11/12/2016
**(JIM WATSON VIA GETTY IMAGES)**

Dear Donald,
Congratulations on your win. I wish you the very best for a successful presidency.

As you know, I supported Clinton. I do not believe in your stated policies, especially your anti-choice stance and your positions on regulation of environmental impacts and healthcare. I think that the Mexicans that are here have improved our society and they should be given a path to citizenship. I do agree that we need stronger borders, but I don't think this can be accomplished with a wall that is unnecessary now and prohibitively costly. But even if you had policies that I could agree with, you do not have the breadth of experience of Clinton; the kind of governing and political experience I think is necessary for the job. Finally, you have changed so much over the time I worked for you and since then that I hardly recognize you from the days we did Trump Tower. You do not have anything like "the best" people working for you and you do not take criticism or listen to advice, two qualities essential to the president.

That is me being honest, and you always told me I was "too honest." But we are where we are, and I am writing you as someone who knew you when. I supported the idea of you becoming president in the 1980s when everyone thought you and I were crazy. At that time, you did have the best people and you followed our advice. Nobody called you Mr. Trump then, we all called you Donald, and you were 100% accessible to us and open to anything we had to say. Your office door was always open and your speakerphone was always on. We paid you deference and treated you with respect, but we were not afraid to be earnest and critical. We did not fear you. You and I know that is not the case with you anymore. You seem to need or want to be adored. Well, you have nothing to prove anymore and you can go back to being a listener willing to change your mind and be corrected. I think fame went to your head and you really started believing you know everything – you don't.

Now you are my president too. Act like it. You have a bunch of losers following you around. The ones in your organization can't do any damage to the country but I can see why you have had so many failures in your business. Now you will be selecting a cabinet and you MUST choose the right people. Show the world that you will only settle for the absolute best.

You should have Republicans and Democrats on your staff and women and people of color. Don't do what the pundits are all predicting.

Giuliani and Gingrich who hang on to you like leeches are out of touch hacks whose time has come and gone. Donald, they are just not worthy of you. Neither is Christie who is despised by the entire state of New Jersey and has zero credibility. The likes of Palin and Carson are also far beneath you. They are cartoon characters, and they are out of touch with most of America. You more than anyone need people who really know governing and politics. Your major concern was always could you trust people. And you put people into positions they didn't deserve because you could trust them, but you must realize that people who would do anything for you are often just holding on to the jobs they know they wouldn't otherwise have. You will find trust worthy people outside your inner circle.

Remember Hillary won the popular vote. More people voted for her than you. These people have priorities that you need to address. You got elected mostly by real people who want their jobs back. True, there are a lot of racists and xenophobes who supported you, but I know you do not really wish to serve their interests. You have your own tendencies which you need to work on. You must be there for the working people of all stripes, and we are not down with the nonsense spewed by most of the people who are pulling at you for appointments. These hacks will only continue the hatred, fear and distrust that were the hallmarks of your campaign.

Get rid of them. You need to shed the image of the Trump supporter who wears a shirt saying Hillary is a cunt, vote for Trump, and replace it with one of the hardworking American, black or white, Christian or Muslim, native or immigrant etc. who is the backbone of the country. Now you are my president too. Act like it.

When I worked for you, you were a democrat. You believed in choice. You supported strong women like me, Susan and Louise. Imagine you glorifying Phyllis Schafley! What must Melania, Ivanka and Rhona think of a woman who said women should not work outside the home? And you want to overturn Roe v. Wade? Why? The country doesn't want this. This will not make you great. Forget it. Remember how you admired, liked and respected Mel Fante, Peter Lobello and Jerry Floyd? You would never tell them they could not get married to the person they love. Forget about overturning gay marriage. You are not like this. Sure Pence would put them all in jail, but that's not you. I suspect he wasn't your first or even close choice for running mate anyway. You say you want to eliminate all regulations, but you don't want to be known as the president that destroyed the environment. You have the opportunity to save the planet because you are the leader of the free world and you have the Congress with you. Protect the earth, the air and the water. You want to repeal Obamacare, but you said yourself that people should have health care. Surprise everyone by coming up with a plan that's better, where people aren't disqualified for pre-existing conditions. It doesn't have to be a plan that business loves. Wall Street expects you to cave to Big Pharma. Astound them by demanding a negotiation on all drug prices. Donald, there is nothing that can stop you.

You can be a president for everyone if you put the country first and let your ego take a back seat. It's hard to respect you after what you have said about women. I have always said you never treated me with discrimination or disrespect, although you did like to leer at pretty women. I wrote that behavior off because of the times, but your conduct on Howard Stern and the Access Hollywood tape is outrageous and cannot be excused. Call it what you want, but it's right there for the world to see. "No one respects women more than I do." What a ridiculous line! But you can be redeemed and you can even win my respect back which I know is very important to you.

First you have to disabuse yourself of the notion that if a woman is harassed she should leave her job. If I did that I would never have gotten to work for you. As a matter of fact, I couldn't have worked anywhere without that treatment in those years. It might help if you admitted that you harassed yourself, and you are ashamed of it. Another thing, don't be flippant about equal pay. This is an important thing and you can have a positive effect. What you need to do is set up a presidential commission on women in industry and have it head up by a real progressive woman who will really study the reasons for pay disparity. You should make it a commitment of your presidency to get women equal pay, get them into non-traditional roles like engineering and construction and, as best as you can, eliminate harassment against them in the workplace. You control all the agencies and can decree changes with an executive order. Oh the great changes you could make for women.

In this crazy world, you are poised to be either a total disaster, or one of the greats. Once you are president, you can do what you want. Forget what it took to get you here. Maybe you will lose some evangelicals and the racists will stay home next time but you will pick up lots of Democrats.

You can be a president for everyone if you put the country first and let your ego take a back seat. Reform the prisons, rebuild our infrastructure, make healthcare affordable, fix immigration humanely. Forget about reducing taxes for the rich, reduce them for the middle class. You know jobs were lost to technology, not to closing factories due to trade agreements. Bring the technology jobs back to the US. Do something about student debt. Help poor young people get college or training for the good jobs you are promising.

I am praying you do some of the things I suggested. I would love to vote for you in 4 years, although I have never voted for a Republican in my life, but I would for you if you changed. I remember the day you bought me a used mink coat when you saw me prancing around the office in it. I remember when you treated me like an equal and we joked around all the time and you called me B. Res and honeybunch. I remember when you consoled me over the fact that the California project got condemned. Even though you totally trashed me I remember the Trump Tower days fondly. I would like to see you go back to the brash, confident and mostly fair person you were then.

When I was on my local school board, I was a real radical. Then they made me president. I rose to the office. I realized that I represented all interests not just my own narrow ones, and I was a better person for it. I know you can be a good president.

---ooo---

# 13.

## Luksa: Dare, Dream, Defy

### Julia Carreon-Lagoc
### Dateline: 11/14/16

I've just heard the most "nagbabagang balita" of the evening, Nov. 8, 2016: the Supreme Court has approved the burial of Dictator Ferdinand Marcos at the Libingan ng Mga Bayani,the National Heroes Cemetery. Heart-breaking news for the victims and survivors of the infamous evil dictatorship: MARCOS MARTIAL LAW. Harrowing details in my column next week.

Meantime, I continue with what I wrote yesterday:

Can you beat the Pinoy? No way, ladies and gentlemen. Who else in the whole wide world are enamored of the longest Christmas season—from September to December? Yup, all the –ber months. September 1, and you hear over the radio Silent Nightto signal the start of the holiday season that may extend 'til first week of the New Year, and a wee bit further.

Long intro, guys and gals. All I wanted to say is that we Pinoy also practice the longest Halloween like what I'm doing right now—Halloween season that begins with the onset of October up to November. And beyond as when relatives from afar arrive to light up the iconic candle for the beloved departed.

Saturday, Oct.22, members of SELDA-Panay (Samahan ng mga Ex-detainees Laban sa Detensyon at Aresto) converged in Plaza Libertad of Iloilo City to celebrate Luksa, Pilipino term for mourning. Big red banner was mounted, titled Mga Martir kag Baganihan sa Paghimakas sang Pumuluyosang Panay. Written on it were 464 names, three of which were that of my brothers—Antonio, Simplicio, Geronimo—and that of my dear departed Rodolfo. Martyrs and heroes honored by friends and relatives in solemn ceremonies with aMass celebrated by Rev. Alfred Candid Jaropillo of UCCP (United Church of Christ in the Philippines). All 464 who, in their time—dare, dream, defy thestatus quo—in the struggle to establish a society that is "just, humane,fraternal" to quote Pope Francis.

**Accents**
**Julia Carreon-Lagoc**
Big 3 little words: "humane, just, fraternal"
We were all glued to the TV as Pope Francis spoke to the U.S. Congress, Sept. 24. It was the Pope's first long-running speech in his six-day visit to America. Three words spoken in succession stuck in my mind: "humane, just, fraternal…" Three words that, to me, vividly encompass all his other speeches.

Humane is another term for caring, kind, compassionate. In his visit to the Philippines last January, Pope Francis' call for mercy and compassion is still fresh in the Filipino mind. He was a picture of gentleness and benevolence. Humane best describes him.

Just is a profound word that demolishes inequality. It is descriptive of an egalitarian society where nobody is deprived of the earth's bounty. Live and let live is the dictum. How can one enjoy unbridled abundance in the face of massive poverty, when three square meals a day is a luxury to many?

Fraternal is to be brotherly which, of course, applies to both men and women, and to all sectors of society that include LGBT —whether or not you are lesbian, gay, bisexual, or transgender. Respect for individual differences is the operative word. We are all brothers and sisters on Mother Earth.

Never before has one person dominated print and broadcast media for nearly a week. The ten presidential contenders of the Republican Party were sidelined by Pope Francis.

From the National Secretariat of the NUPL (National Union of Peoples' Lawyers) this immense quote in honor of human rights lawyers: "By calling yourselves the 'people's lawyer,' you have made a remarkable choice. You decided not to remain in the sidelines. Where human rights are assaulted, you have chosen to sacrifice the comfort of the fence for the dangers of the battlefield. But only those who choose to fight on the battlefield live beyond irrelevance." - Supreme Court Chief Justice Reynato S. Puno, in his message at the NUPL Founding Congress, September 15, 2007. Chief Justice Puno explicitly and convincingly expressed why human rights lawyers are no fence-sitters. They take sides and fight for a just, egalitarian, democratic society.

From the late Atty. Romeo T. Capulong, NUPL founding chairperson, in his keynote address at the Fifth Conference of Lawyers in Asia Pacific, September 18, 2010: "After long years of experience as a people's lawyer, I can honestly say it has been a treasured journey of self-fulfillment and rewarding achievement. I know it will be the same for all others who choose to tread this path." Like Chief Justice Puno, Atty. Capulong remains an inspiration to human rights lawyers.

May I ask for your indulgence, dear reader, with this paragraph I wrote in 2012, seven days before my husband Rudy breathed his last: "January 30, 2012, doctors and nurses asked how long we've been married when they saw the balloons beautifully imprinted: Happy Anniversary! Well, well, it was our 52nd wedding anniversary. Fifty-two years of hard labor, huh? What is the tie that binds? Excess of patience? What mettle? Hey, folks, say what you will, the tie that binds is harmony in aims and values. Similarity of interests is saying it lightly. Guts and grit in us would be stronger — to deflect the slings and arrows of outrageous fortune, if we have to be Shakespearean about it. I could think of only one word that bound us for 52 years. The word is activists. Yes, Rudy and I are both activists, and always will be (he across the Great Divide). I could imagine him shaking hands with the comrades who, like him, also went ahead. Comrades with their dreams and hopes for the people—the dispossessed, the disempowered, the oppressed and exploited—struggling for a better life." A married life followed by eventual death.

Now you know why I lighted a candle in Luksa. juliaclagoc@yahoo.com

---oOo---

# 14.

# The 2016 US Presidential Elections
## Honorio M. Cruz
(hmcruzmd@gmail.com posted at
Moonglowplanet and worldwide-Filipino
Alliance@yahoogroups.com)
Dateline: 3 November 2016

It's took about a year and a half since the preliminaries started, billions of dollars spent and characterized as one of the dirtiest of all times, the gloves came off during the nominating process, especially on the Republican side. The weeding out process with 17 candidates joining the fray, the number probably buoyed by the prospect of squaring off with a flawed candidate and a 65% disapproval of the direction the country is headed, a repudiation of Obama's two terms of stewardship.

Sixteen of these candidates were with impressive resumes, but another however was a rookie, never having thrown his hat in the ring before, a billionaire businessman, with a reputation of getting things done below budget and ahead of time. He was regarded as a lightweight, having ingratiated himself with his Birther theory of Obama, years after most people have moved on. He however emerged, by billing himself as the ultimate outsider, brawling his way through, getting himself in the battle of all battles where tact and decorum were thrown out of the window, where bruised egos and fatal wounds were inflicted. Some of the wounds were never designed to be healed, resulting in a fractured party like no other in the recent times, where coming back home at the end was too wide a gap to be breached.

At the end of the weeding out process, his rivals with the exception of a few, retreated in their own corner and didn't come back to the center of the ring to congratulate him for having won. The gentlemen's sport was no longer gentle, nor was it just among men, two women joined the fray, one from each side.

On the Democratic side the lady warrior, was a veteran of many wars, the ultimate insider, with an impressive resume of around 20 years of public service ranging from being the First Lady for the Governor of a small state, leaping on to being the First Lady of the White House, then became a Senator of the big state of New York, a failed candidacy for the Presidency, but moving on to the Secretary of State for 4 years. In all those years, she never took her eye off the crown, her dreams of shattering that glass ceiling as the first female President of the US. It was temporarily shunted aside for 8 years when another ceiling was broken, the First Black President.

This time around, she would not be denied, with over a billion dollars of war chest and a collection of pygmies for the preliminary bouts, limited by the prospect of squaring off against the Clinton legacy and machinery and oodles of money, scaring off no less than the two term Vice President of Obama.

Indeed, it was a collection of tomato fighters which folded after the first jabs were thrown, like stage managed bouts. Weaklings as they were, the first sign of a chink in her armor was her inability to knock off an old senile looking fighter (Senator Sanders), whose main credential was to promise free cookies for everybody. He was supposed to take a fall in the early rounds, and why not, the promoters, the judges and the referee were all in cahoots with the lady warrior, but he fooled them all, managing to win many rounds, late in the bout. Too bad for the old guy, the judges had reserved the last rounds just in case it was needed for her to win the bout. Ever a gracious guy, he meekly conceded before the end of the bout, to the consternation of his diehard fans, who learned that the fix was in. Firing the promoter, but replacing her with another, more crooked than the first, was not enough to soothe the Berne supporters. Feeling betrayed, many vowed not to vote for Hillary or join third party candidates.

When the victors from the primaries entered the ring for the main event, one came out bloodied, all alone with no entourage, booed by his own party as he was introduced. On the other hand the lady boxer came out smelling like a rose, all perfumed, lipstick and rouge to hide the facial imperfections and her lone rival enthusiastically cheering her on for the bout. The immediate and ensuing odds was of course a no brainer, the money was over-whelmingly for the lady boxer to slay the wounded, lonely warrior, who immediately got himself into trouble using expletives and bombast as he waded into the ring, thinking that he was still fighting with his fellow locker room mates. A rude awakening! He suddenly realized that the women in the audience outnumbered men and preferred gentlemen warriors and his lady opponent would capitalize on this fact pleading victimhood, and a women champion for their cause, a rallying cry to burst through that glass ceiling, for what else could she point to as an accomplishment in the past 20 years as an ultimate insider and mover. Indeed she is more remembered for her colossal failures in the foreign policy which she authored.

In the early probing rounds The Donald landed some self-inflicted wounds through his mouth and twitter and voices from his past, re-enforcing the lady warrior's charge that he is a sexual predator, with the help of the Clinton's smear machine parading "victims", keeping the Donald preoccupied in preventing those blows from tarnishing his carefully managed image, rather than talking about the major issues confronting the country. Abandoned by the leadership of his party and perceived as an anchor too heavy a burden to carry, the Donald had to do the heavy lifting all on his own against both the Clinton Gang, the Democratic Machinery, the biased media and the glitterati. His slash and burn technique endeared him to his core supporters but alienated almost everybody else, his untimely tweets and off the cuff remarks from the past haunted him through the whole campaign, women suddenly emerged from the shadows to tar him and Gloria Allred had her stable of female Trump bashers resulting in low poll ratings and worse, a highly unfavorable rating, even lower than the Queen Bee herself.

With all her history of scandals, resulting in prison terms for her cohorts, reenforced by her inexplicable actions in deleting government related Emails done with an unlawful private server, after receiving a subpoena from Congress to preserve those documents, were damning. Indeed there were suspicious and highly classified materials that passed through her private server. Unlawfully deleting them is a crime that aroused suspicion that those Emails contained highly dubious materials which Hill and Bill have committed through the auspices of the Clinton Foundation, charged by her detractors as a giant pay to play scheme extorting funds in the tens of millions of dollars to fill the coffers of the Foundation and their personal fortune. Plenty of smokes but no smoking gun, according to the FBI Director Comey, clearing her of crime, although excoriating her for being extremely careless with classified materials and admitting that she lied in Congress numerous times on direct questioning by Rep. Trey Gowdy. How could one recover from such an indictment while clearing her of a crime, reenforcing her image as untrustworthy, but she did, never even going below Trumps ratings through all her troubles.

The ebb and flow of the main event was predictably boring for those who closely followed the primaries, ammunitions gathered during those preliminary bouts were quickly spent. Both fatally flawed candidates, would not have survived the preliminaries, were there anyone who knew how to fight dirty and at the same time tap in to the sentiments of the disaffected silent majority, who have endured 8 years of being marginalized by both the major parties, many ostracized by the prodigious extreme left machine including the media elite, branding them as racist, misogynist, greedy politically incorrect, in short a basket of deplorables, so aptly labeled by Hillary and more disappointingly, disowned by their own party for enunciating what they felt in their heart was true, seeing their love for old American values as un-American. They have become the new Tea Party Deplorables, only this time silent, uncounted for in poll after polls, witnessed by the overwhelming crowds in Trump rallies, yet showed him trailing in the polls, never going above Hillary's through the election day. How sweet was redemption day, when finally their votes were counted, no longer silent, they spoke loud and clear. The traditional blue wall was shattered, give credit to Trump who tapped into theses cracks and turned them red. For a while traditional politicians were labeling him crazy for sniffing at the wrong trees, expending resources best used in the traditional battleground states. He did those and then some, criss-crossing the country and logging in many thousands of miles in the last few days 3-4 rallies a day, all with overwhelming crowds, an energizer bunny on steroids, while Hillary, secure in her machinery and surrogates sparingly extended herself, until the last week when the Trump Train started to bear down and the Clanton Gang called all the kings horses and all the king's men, the gliteratti, the crowd gatherers, singers, actors and and actresses and even the King himself enthusiastically campaigned to keep the Queen Bee shining with the help of her adoring media. Even the pollsters joined in the facade sometimes tweaking the numbers by overweighting the Democrats in the poll responders.

On the day of the elections, the early returns weren't too encouraging for the Trumpers, projected by the pundits and pollsters to be needing an inside straight to have a chance to win, Florida and North

Carolina, even Ohio seemed uncertain. It was a blessing that we were in a cruise at the Mexican Riviera when the election returns started coming in, time to dig into the sumptuous dinner and wash away the specter of four more years of Democratic rule, all 8 of us Trump supporters, meekly admitting the inevitable. The dinner lasted a little over an hour and as we prepare to go to the disco and show, a quick peek at the TV showed stunned TV anchors surmising that the tables have turned and that Hillary will need an inside straight to have a chance. Trump was ahead at 216 electoral votes and leading in most of the contested states, in spite of California and Oregon having gone to her column, Michigan and Pennsylvania, traditional blue states were purple at that moment. What a pleasant surprise, and the pundits and pollsters were starting to eat their words and uttering *mea culpas.* It was like a tea party resurgence only made up of a different mixture and unannounced, undetected. In the end the whole electoral map was a sea of red and the dreaded Trump anchor became coat tails for the Senators and the Congressmen who lost but a few seats and instead of losing both houses, preserved them, and with the White House in tow, they have control of two branches of the government and a chance to at least replace one staunch conservative for the Supreme Court. A couple of Liberals in the court, aged beyond their usefulness will have to be persuaded or be mummified in their bench to keep their seat, El Cid on his horse.

The subsequent days were full of recrim-inations and self-flagellation for the pollsters and pundits, and even the venerable old lady, The New York Times apologized to Trump and her readers, that henceforth, she would treat the elected President fairly. How about following her own motto by printing "all the news that is fit to print" and leave the editorials and bias reporting less tilted to the left. It is remarkable that as usual, after a bitter defeat, the Democrats and their adherents refused to recognize the victor and would like to change the rules of the game, after it finished and they lost, advocating a do-over in a different rule, some reserving the right to recognize the loser as the winner. Some anarchists saw the opportunity and joined the rallies and the one in Oregon burning cars breaking into and looting establishments. How ironic that they themselves predicted the Trumpers to be doing the very same thing that they are presently doing. Never mind that Trump won 306 electoral votes, one sinister opiner in these fora even suggested that the electors vote against Trump and some erstwhile fact checkers even grasping from thin air that Hillary won by 6 million popular votes. Some would like to secede from the USA, taking the blue states in the West Coast. It might not be too farfetched, a catclysmic cough from the San Andreas fault might just grant their wish. Well, anyway, guys, COOL IT!!! Or if unconsolable, drink your Kool Ade. It's not the end of the world. You might even enjoy it...HMC

---oOo---

# 15.

## An Egg for a GI
### A memoir

### Fred Natividad
Dateline: Revised 7/13/2010

It came about that we – a group of families in our neighborhood of Lumbaan - evacuated to a village called Dalongue, just about a mile northwest of our town proper. I don't know who chose Dalongue as our evacuation center.

Nor do I know who spread the welcome news that American liberation forces will hit Lingayen Gulf beaches, eight miles north of us, on January 9, 1945, with the warning that our hometown, including our own neighborhood of Lumbaan, will be bombarded by the Americans because of intelligence that our town was crawling with Japanese. The intelligence was false but the Americans rained shells on the town anyway. Our house did not suffer a direct hit but the shell that fell on the front yard peppered the porous front facade of the flimsy bamboo structure. It was a good thing that we fled our neighborhood for Dalongue.

We did not see the landings but we saw the skies over Lingayen Gulf from the safety of Dalongue. We saw black balls of smoke pop all over the distant Lingayen Gulf skies, unaware at first that they came out of American anti-aircraft guns staving off Japanese suicide planes trying to dive into U.S. Navy ships.

Anyway, maybe a day or two after the landings, we were still in Dalongue and to our great curiosity, we saw American soldiers walking on the rice fields walking south towards Sonkil or Balingueo. They may have come from the town proper and judging from their few numbers of about a dozen GI's they may have been an advance patrol of squad size.

I remember that they walked forward without avoiding mud puddles. Yet they didn't seem to be on the alert nor were they in a hurry as they silently walked while staring at us who lined their path. We also stared back at them with quiet whispers, marveling at what appeared to us as their incredible, giant heights compared to our average Filipino height of five feet, four inches.

They slung their weapons on their shoulders, obviously confident that there were no Japanese in the area. It will be years later for me to presume, based on a book on the history of the Lingayen Gulf landings, that they were from the 20th Infantry, 6th Division, I Corps, of General Krueger's Sixth Army. The 20th Infantry reached Balingueo two days after landing at Lingayen Gulf.

From our whispering crowd, one of our elders came up with an idea to welcome the soldiers. Maybe it was my grandfather, our Lumbaan neighborhood elder (they called him a "teniente del barrio" in those days), who asked someone to fetch an egg for me to give to the nearest GI.

I cringed. Compared to my younger brother (who was seven months short of being six and I was seven months short of being twelve), I was timid. Then our crowd, no longer whispering, dared my younger brother if he can do what I can't do.

He couldn't resist the challenge, the braggart. He hesitated a bit, then he grabbed the egg and ran quickly to one of the soldiers. He handed the egg without a word to a surprised GI. He was about to run back to us in triumph when the GI grabbed and lifted the now scared boy up and happily took him around to the other soldiers.

The soldiers actually stopped their patrol and fussed around the boy talking merrily among themselves in their strange accents that we were not used to hear. Three or four GI's groped in their pockets for sticks of gum, chocolates, and a few sticks of cigarettes which they then gave to my brother. We didn't understand a word they said because of their twangy accents, but we knew they were appreciative of the symbolic welcome of one raw, puny egg.

Then they sent the boy back to us, waved goodbye to everybody and resumed their leisurely patrol.

The adults lit up all five sticks of cigarettes at once. For each cigarette four or five adults took puffing turns. How they savored the long lost, aromatic American smoke that they missed for three atrocious years of Japanese occupation! What my brother got for one puny egg gave so much pleasure to about fifteen people!

We kids, of course, under the supervision of an adult, shared the chocolate bars and the sticks of chewing gum - one tiny bit for each of the dozen or so children who shared three chocolate bars and five pieces of Wrigley's chewing gum.

My braggart brother was a hero for some weeks!

I never dreamed that about two decades hence I would be gawking at a Chicago landmark on Michigan Avenue: The Wrigley Building. It is the headquarters of the company that made Wrigley's chewing gum, the same gum so novel for kids who have forgotten the joy of chewing gum for three years, the same gum that was an unintended trade for one puny egg for a GI.

Come to think of it - I do not remember chewing gum sold in stores during the Japanese occupation.

Fred Natividad@2008 Livonia, Michigan

*Fred Natividad Posting from historic Virginia   =Say nanlapuan lingawen pian antay arapen.  =Alamin ang pinang-galingan upang malaman ang paro-roonan. =Know where we had been to guide us where we are going.*

---oOo---

# 16.

## Rodrigo Duterte: Back to the Future

### Allen Gaborro
Dateline: November 14, 2016

A common thread that I am finding in the responses to my criticisms of Philippine president Rodrigo Duterte is that I should give the man a chance before I drive hard against his words and actions. Respondents have suggested instead that I reallocate my energies for a much later time when we would be better able to assess and evaluate Duterte's performance.

The reasoning that has been put forth by these respondents as they take issue with my criticism of the Philippine president converges on a frame of reference which is centered around the overdue need for reform. However, the way the respondents have defended that frame of reference is incompatible with one of the important lessons of analyzing political leaders: ignore the past at your peril for it is ever-present in the ways and means of how rulers will exercise power.

The last thing Duterte supporters want to hear is that the most vociferous in their praise of him run the risk of becoming the most vociferous in their disapproval of the president down the road. As they applaud him for his ruthlessly violent stance against drug-related crime—as if in and of itself killing suspected drug users and dealers alone will stop drug crime in the country—Duterte supporters constantly remind us that "change" is what it's all about and that only he can carry out that change as a leader who is tough and strong and who will do what is in the best interests of the Filipino people.

But what the Duterte supporters ignore is the historical truism that how someone comes to power will be exactly the way they will rule once in power. To put it differently, the past is a valuable resource in prognosticating the future with Duterte at the helm of the country.

Duterte's political past raises many eyebrows for his alleged involvement in the so-called Davao death squads which are believed to have extra-judicially taken the lives of hundreds of people in the city for crimes, real and imagined. Duterte has freely and without remorse admitted his complicity in the killings and has even bragged about their bloody effectiveness in reducing crime in Davao.

But in using excessive lethal force without due process of law undermines the very notion of law and order that forms Duterte's political center of gravity. To circumvent the rule of law in order to enforce law and order is an example of the narrow sophistry and rationalizing that is a trademark of President Duterte's governing style. Maintaining law and order by breaking it is the height of hypocrisy and the absence of common sense and reason. Duterte however, has parlayed this into a winning narrative among his voters.

There is something to be said for the overall conclusion that Duterte has reached on the U.S.-Philippine relationship. Since its genesis in the turn-of-the-century American colonization of the archipelago, it has been a hegemonic patron-client relationship to be sure and on that account Filipino nationalists have said that Duterte is justified in reliving the painful memories of how it has— materially, physically, culturally, and psychologically—highlighted American strength and at the same time underscored Philippine weakness and dependency.

A singular take-home for Duterte from the history of the US-Philippine relationship is his near-scathing indignation at a specific episode in America's historically-checkered role in the islands. It involved a 2002 explosion in the Davao hotel room of Michael Terrence Meiring, a US citizen who had been indicted for possessing explosives. Before any case could be pursued, Meiring mysteriously disappeared. Davao mayor Duterte believed that the US government had somehow wielded its magical wand of neo-colonial machinations in enabling Meiring to escape justice. Duterte has understandably never forgotten that incident. Indeed, what has become a ritual response for Duterte in his critical scrutiny of America's constructive yet controversial history in the Philippines has been laced with defiance and bitterness and filled with invective towards the former colonizer and long-time patron.

A far more distant historical event that Duterte talks about with rancor is the massacre of 600 Moros at the hands of American soldiers in 1906. Hardly one to expound upon the necessity of forgiveness when acting as the protagonist, Duterte has demanded an apology from the United States for the massacre which took place on Jolo Island in the southernmost reaches of the Philippine island chain. What became known as the Bud Dajo massacre occurred against the backdrop of

America's counterinsurgency operations against Moro rebels who resisted the colonial occupation of their land.

Duterte has tried to sear these two historical moments—along with his general enmity towards the United States—into the contemporary Filipino consciousness to the same pathological extent he has carved it into his own. And yet, Duterte does so with great irony. About the president and his insights on the United States, novelist Gina Apostol writes: "An abuser condemned an earlier abuser of the nation in order to sanction his own abuse."

Duterte has been able to project his antipathy towards the US government's neo-colonial policies into a national policy of his own. It is a policy that is slowly turning US-Philippine relations on their head. It is also a policy loaded with a range of unintended consequences not the least of which is the appeasement of a repressive dictatorship in China. China, with its exertive ambitions on maritime territories in the South China Sea—some of which are legally under Philippine sovereignty—potentially represents a clear and present danger to the Philippines.

One only has to open their eyes to Duterte's political past as a brutally honest, uncompromising mayor and presidential aspirant to see how it informs his thought processes as president. The atrocious acts of guilty-until-proven-innocent violence perpetrated against thousands of suspected drug dealers and users and his precipitous disruption of vital US-Philippine ties both arise out of the recesses of his public past.

The problem with the Duterte defenders that I have heard from is that they disregard what his past has to say about how he would conduct himself as president. It was Duterte after all, who as a mayor and presidential candidate advocated extrajudicial killings—irrespective of any human collateral damage—to fight the drug trade. It was mayor Duterte who shouted from the mountaintop his aversion towards America and who as presidential candidate telegraphed that he was willing to jeopardize relations with the United States—an impeachable but indispensable ally nevertheless—for both historical and personal affronts. It was candidate Duterte who threatened to abolish the Philippine Congress if its members did not facilitate the passage of his policies. And it was first as mayor and then as presidential candidate that Duterte unconscionably called for the burial of former dictator Ferdinand Marcos as an undeserved national hero.

Nothing that Duterte says and does consequentially as president, now and in the future, cannot be traced back to the record of his dubious, pseudo-democratic public past, a past that has been glossed over with his populist, anti-establishment, everyman image by his hordes of disaffected supporters.

The respondents' sentiment that at any rate—his contentious past notwithstanding—Duterte is an agent of change so therefore he's better than no change at all is the definition of self-deception. Change has to be implemented responsibly, compassionately, and sensibly. To implement it thoughtlessly and full speed ahead simply for the sake of change itself is going too far, too fast. In other words, the cure should not be worse than the disease. Change is only a salutary preoccupation if it is sown with unmistakable empathy and judiciously maximized to such a fundamental level as to be truly meaningful.

When the regrets start pouring in over the course of time with Rodrigo Duterte, it will be too late. The damage will have been done. Then Filipinos will hit themselves over the head as they ask themselves, as they did with Marcos, Estrada, and Macapagal-Arroyo, and with countless other politicians, why they enabled these individuals, individuals they knew in their hearts to have questionable ethics and morals, to rise to the pinnacle of power.

---oOo---

# 17.

## Duterte Won't Declare Martial Law; He Doesn't Have To

### Rodel Rodis
Dateline: Nov. 15, 2016,
http: globalnation.inquirer.net

I am absolutely confident that Pres. Rodrigo Duterte will not declare martial law. This confidence is based on the bountiful evidence that the Filipino people seem entirely too willing to voluntarily surrender their fundamental constitutional rights so there would be no need to formally declare martial law.

This conclusion is drawn from the public reaction to a speech Pres. Duterte delivered at the regional convention of the Integrated Bar of the Philippines (IBP) on November 4. In that Manila Hotel speech, Duterte informed his audience of lawyers that there will be a massive demonstration against him in the United States next year and that the moving force behind this protest is Filipino American Loida Nicolas-Lewis.

"Meron next year, a certain financier, mayaman na babae who married a black and is now a millionaire and she is planning to do massive demonstration," he said.

An online publication, politics.com.ph reported Duterte's speech in its November 4, 2016 issue with this sensationalized banner headline:

"**Duterte unmasks Loida Nicolas Lewis' plot to launch massive protests to oust him**."

If that report is true, is that a crime? If not, why did Duterte feel the need to "unmask" Loida?

**IS ORGANIZING A PROTEST RALLY A CRIME?**

The Philippine lawyers at that convention, as well as Duterte himself, who was a former government prosecutor, are all aware of Article III Section 4 of the 1987 Philippine Constitution which states that "No law shall be passed abridging the freedom of speech, of expression, or of the press, or the right of the people peaceably to assemble and petition the government for redress of grievances".

The IBP members are also familiar with the Philippine case of <u>Jacinto vs. Court of Appeal</u> [346 SCRA 665 (1997)] which held that the right to peaceably assemble and petition for redress of grievances is, together with freedom of speech, of expression and of the press, "a right that enjoy primacy in the realm of constitutional protection. For these rights constitute the very basis of a functional democratic policy, without which all the other rights would be meaningless and unprotected."

But yet none of the Philippine lawyers at the Manila Hotel on Nov. 4 stood up to defend Loida Nicolas Lewis, who placed 7th in the Philippine bar exams in 1967, and who was the first Filipina to be admitted to practice law in New York state. None dared to assert to Pres. Duterte that Loida has every right to call for a peaceful demonstration against Duterte even if it is "massive".

One Philippine attorney stood up for Loida. In his Internet post, former senator Rene Saguisag wrote that he has known Loida since the early 1960s when they were both involved in the Student Catholic Action (SCA) and in the National Union of Students (NUS) and when they "bar-reviewed" together in San Beda in 1967 although Loida went to the University of the Philippines School of Law.

"I know that if Loida wants something done," Saguisag wrote, "she will do it by the force of reason and never by reason of force. She'll do it morally and legally… No mean bone in a kind and gentle soul."

Saguisag expressed concern that a few of Duterte's followers may be "unhinged" and that therefore "Loida needs to be more careful here, where she spends a lot of time, doing good, or elsewhere." The former senator wondered "how the lawyers in that Integrated Bar of the Philippines assembly responded when the Prez, willy-nilly, casually put lawyer Loida's safety in jeopardy, by convicting her by publicity."

"We have to have a higher regard for human life and dignity," Saguisag counselled.

## CAUSE FOR SAGUISAG'S CONCERN

There is good reason for Saguisag to be concerned for Loida's safety. After Duterte's attack against Loida appeared online, Duterte's numerous supporters in the social media immediately began trolling Loida in their Facebook pages.

One such Duterte supporter, Mira Savaria Encabo, an OFW based in Bahrain, posted this Facebook blast against Loida Nicolas Lewis:

"**She is the Mouthpiece of America but posturing a facade of Filipino patriot. How can she be a pro-Filipino when all her businesses are in the US and all her allegiance is to the American flag??? Can we let a Fil-Am whose** only claim to fame is her being married to a rich African-American and who doesn't even have the guts to bring or donate even a little portion of her wealth and money to Philippines to help the government and the poor???

What had she done to help the country and have the guts to organize a destabilization move and to OUST THE BEST PRESIDENT PHILIPPINES EVER HAD IN THE RECENT HISTORY???? ALL SHE DID IS TALKING TOO MUCH and going for TV INTERVIEWS! Pretending to be the voice of the people!!!

What right does she have to meddle in Philippine affairs when she lives comfortably in US, sheltered from all the trappings of life in the Philippines while she enjoys the luxury of her late husband's wealth????

Why can't she concentrate campaigning against discrimination and racism which the blacks are still experiencing in US? It would definitely make her late husband's soul to rejoice knowing his money is being spent in something worth fighting for rather than spending it trying to demoralize, destabilize and throw out the government and PRESIDENCY LEGALLY ELECTED by the PEOPLE!!!"

It is evident that the Duterte supporter never bothered to google search "Loida Nicolas Lewis" and relied entirely on Duterte's false description of her as simply "mayaman na babae who married a black and is now a millionaire."

## THE TRUTH ABOUT LOIDA NICOLAS LEWIS

If any of them had bothered to do basic research, they would have learned that Loida was already a lawyer when she met Reginald F. Lewis (not "Richard") on a blind date in New York City in 1968 when he graduated from Harvard Law School, and that they were married a year later in Manila.

They lived in a condo in Manhattan while raising their two daughters with Loida employed as a lawyer for the Immigration and Naturalization Service (INS) while Reginald was working for a top New York law firm. After 15 years as a corporate lawyer, Reginald formed his own venture capital firm in 1983, TLC Group L.P., which he then used to purchase Beatrice International Foods in 1987 which became the first black-owned company to have more than $1 billion in annual sales.

In 1993, Reginald Lewis died of cerebral hemorrhage from brain cancer. A year later, Loida was picked by the Board of Directors to be the CEO and chair of the board of TLC Beatrice, a post she held until 2000. As CEO, she cut costs and sold non-core and under-performing assets, reduced liabilities and strengthened the management team. In October 1995, Loida was named the top US business executive by the National Foundation for Women Business Owners and Working Woman Magazine.

Also, contrary to the misinformation being spread on social media by Duterte supporters, Loida has invested heavily in the Philippines including founding and operating The Lewis College in Sorsogon which offers quality education in accountancy and business as well as in science and technology, providing scholarships to the poor students of her home province of Sorsogon.

As chair of US Pinoys for Good Governance, Loida Nicolas Lewis, a dual citizen of the US and the

Philippines, has also championed the cause of Philippine sovereignty in the West Philippine Sea leading global protests against the Chinese invasion in Philippine territorial waters. She has called for a global boycott of goods made in China making her "China's Public Enemy #1".

The malicious attacks on Loida Nicolas Lewis by Duterte on November 4 were not aimed at just silencing Loida but were directed at discouraging Filipino Americans from joining protest demonstrations against his administration.

**THE MESSAGE FOR FILIPINOS IN THE PHILIPPINES**

For the Filipinos in the Philippines, the message was delivered the following day on November 5 when more than a dozen fully-armed members of the Criminal Investigation and Detection Group of Eastern Visayas (CIDG-8) arrived at the provincial jail cell of Albuera, Leyte Mayor Rolando Espinosa at around 4 a.m. "to serve a search warrant" on him. They removed all the jail guards and proceeded to shoot and kill Espinosa and his cell mate.

Columnist Solita Monsod described the police officers' cover story as "so flimsy it was evident that the police were confident that they would get away with it."

Sure enough, a week later, Duterte announced that he believed the version of events presented by the police, whatever it is, as incredible as it may be. Duterte reiterated his promise to protect cops from being charged if the cases filed against them came while they were doing their duty.

As Rigoberto Tiglao commented in his Manila Times column on November 13, 2016: "Duterte's stance means we no longer have a rule of law in this country but the rule of a President and his police who can execute anybody they want, and claim that their target had fought it out and the police didn't have any choice but to defend themselves."

"The CIDG-8 demonstrated how the police can undertake such execution with total impunity and brazenness that we should all be outraged, not only at such trampling of our rule of law, but at such ruthless, merciless murder carried out by supposed agents of the law," Tiglao wrote.

So, it's good news, bad news. The good news is that Pres. Duterte will not declare martial law. The bad news is that no one would notice it now if he did.

*(Send comments to Rodel50@gmail.com or mail them to the Law Offices of Rodel Rodis at 2429 Ocean Avenue, San Francisco, CA 94127).*

---ooo---

# 18.

## The Natural Bridge
## a travelogue

### Fred Natividad
### Dateline: 2015

Way back before her wedding, my niece Ayreen and her husband Jonas, came across a park in the middle of nowhere in southwest Virginia. It is called Natural Bridge because its main feature is a naturally formed limestone arch. They decided to have their wedding there.

It is now a state park but prior to becoming one it was privately owned for two and a half centuries. Among some former owners was a historically eminent character named Thomas Jefferson. In the fall of 2015 Jonas and Ayreen set their wedding. At the time the Virginia Conservation Legacy Fund, a civic outfit, still owned the park but it intended to donate it to Virginia.

The park's main attraction, obviously, is the natural limestone arch that towers a couple hundred feet above slow flowing Cedar Creek. Along with a 152-room hotel, the park sits on 1,540 acres of rural Virginia. A Native American village of the Monacan tribe has been recreated as an additional tourist attraction along with underground caverns 34 feet down. There are also hiking trails for visitors. We did not have a chance to visit the village, the caverns or the hiking trails.

Natural Bridge Park is accessible by way of I-64 and I-81. In fact, going there is chiefly by driving. But if one is not a "local," (relatives and friends who attended the wedding were not "locals"), one may need first to fly by commercial airline either to Washington DC or to Richmond Virginia and then drive on to Natural Bridge. The national capital, Washington DC, has three airports while Richmond, the state capital of Virginia,100 miles south on I-95 has an international airport. The drive from the airports will take between three to four hours.

Since we are "locals" we didn't fly. Kikay and I drove from Fredericksburg, our current American hometown after a number of moves from one town to another in three states. Fredericksburg is located on I-95 halfway between the two capitals - Washington, DC, and Richmond, Virginia. Our son Philip, his wife Jenny and their girls Sana and Annika drove separately in two cars.

From Fredericksburg it may normally take three hours to drive southwestward to Natural Bridge but Kikay and I drove at leisurely pace. We cut through country roads and it took us four hours to negotiate 150 miles. We were, however, amply rewarded with lovely views of the countryside - quiet farms, solitary farm houses far apart from each other, glimpses of small ranches bordered by woods along winding roads on sometimes hilly terrain. We think these bucolic scenes of Virginia's southwestern hinterlands are a microcosm of America's productive farms.

Ayreen, a social worker and a Washington DC transplant, was raised in far away Long Beach, California. Her husband Jonas, an engineer, is from nearby Delaware. Before their wedding Ayreen thought that Jonas, being an engineer, may have been fascinated by the bridge-like limestone arch. Most probably the couple simply fell in love with the remote beauty of the place. Being so out of the way may have preserved the park's postcard bucolic setting.

The park is awash with history which I did not know about when we came for Ayreen's wedding. With further readings I came to know later some stories about Natural Bridge. Legend has it that the Native American Monacan tribe was already there for centuries before any white frontiersman set foot on the area in the 18th century. Another legend is that a young George Washington once surveyed the area for some British official.

What may be a true story and not merely a legend is that the legendary Thomas Jefferson, before he became president, bought this property from some British royalty for $160 two years before the United States declared its independence from the Brits. It would be interesting to know what today's equivalent is of the $160 of those old days.

Natural Bridge has been a vacation spot since Thomas Jefferson reportedly built a log cabin on the property which he used as a vacation house and in which he entertained dignitaries while he was president. The place must have been already popular that early in its history because even Europeans crossed The Big Pond and then stuffered inland horseback rides or rode horse drawn carriages to visit. Cadillacs and Jaguars were not yet in existence for wealthy European tourists. Another history tidbit is that in the vicinity of Natural Bridge is the "Lost River" whose water was used in extracting nitrate for the manufacture of ammunition in the war of 1812.

Fast forward to the autumn of 2015… On the eve of their wedding Jonas and Ayreen hosted a prenuptial dinner. It was not the usual prenuptial dinners we have attended. It was held at a restaurant that was not merely brewery-themed but is actually inside a real brewery in the middle of nowhere, complete with real brewery smells. A restaurant in a brewery in the middle of nowhere? Well, I thought it is in the middle of nowhere because we are used to the urban ambience of Fredericksburg located between two urban capital cities. Not surprisingly there was ample beer with the food but we …hic… managed to stay sober when it was time to get back to our hotels for the night.

A minister officiated the wedding by the Cedar Creek over which the huge natural bridge loomed. It must have been quite a sight that we were in our best finery in contrast to the casual vacation garb of tourists coming and going. Even the Caucasian minister wore a barong in cognizance of Ayreen's Filipino roots although Jonas has Gaelic roots. It was not a Catholic wedding but relatives managed to incorporate at least two customs - the veil and coin ceremonies - common at Filipino Catholic weddings. I was assigned to hand over a quarter to Jonas during the rites for the coin ceremony but the bride's mother, my sister Doniang, replaced it with 13 coins traditionally used in Filipino weddings.

Why 13 coins? One of my departed aunts once said the number 13 was to memorialize the 13 faces at The Last Supper.

A photographer had, among his gadgets, a camera-toting drone which he flew over us. He got careless. A park like this is thick with trees and he drove his drone into one of the trees. The drone got snagged on one tree. As he extricated it with a remote controller it came tumbling down crackling with sparks. Fortunately this happened after the ceremonies. That would have been an unwelcome commotion while Ayreen and Jonas were solemnly exchanging their "I do's".

There is a large hall at the park has a lounge with dining tables and chairs. Part of the lounge is open to a wide patio along the creek. The patio is an extension of the dining lounge which is furnished with outdoor dining table and chairs. Tours usually start out from this hall but for their wedding Jonas and Ayreen hired the place as a snack room with a bar. While I lined up for a shot of whiskey it occurred to me that since we arrived for this wedding we had been spending a lot of time eating and drinking! Not long after we had our snacks we climbed into the bus that shuttled us to the big hotel for the reception.

Another date with food and drinks!

Anyway, aside from the banquet and dancing and drinking for the toasts we enjoyed intimate hobnobbing with the new in-laws of Ayreen. We pinned a dollar or two on Jonas during the dollar dance after which we retired to our motel.

We, from Fredericksburg, checked into a small motel less fancier than the hotel where the reception was to be held and where most of the other guests checked in. Kikay and I got a big scare when we discovered in the morning that Philip and his family were not in their room, yet one of their two cars was still parked in front. After several frantic calls trying to locate them they finally responded. They spent the night at the house that the bride's family rented in Buchanan, ten miles away. There the girls, Sana, Annika and their California cousins, Athena and Angelique, shucked the long gowns they wore as members of the wedding entourage. Other relatives also got rid of tuxedoes and gowns after which they continued celebrating.

The rented house is located a few meters away from the bank of the James River in tiny Buchanan town. It is a vintage house quite big enough that it can sleep 20 people as long as some would not mind sleeping on several sofas and stuffy big chairs, or on the floor in sleeping bags or on bunk beds in the basement.

Buchanan is a tourist attraction in that part of Virginia remotely away from Washington DC, the prime destination of tourists to Virginia and Maryland. Buchanan is a quaint small town with souvenir shops on its short main street. An outfit operates a canoe rental at the river bank behind the house. After a picnic style breakfast at the house (here we go again with food!) Sana, Annika and their other cousins stayed to go canoeing while others got into their rental cars and headed for the airport to catch their flights to Chicago and California or elsewhere.

Too old for canoeing, Kikay and I drove home enjoying the fall foliage along I-81 and I-64.

*Fred Natividad Posting from historic Virginia   =Say nanlapuan lingawen pian antay arapen.  =Alamin ang pinang-galingan upang malaman ang paro-roonan. =Know where we had been to guide us where we are going.*

---oOo---